METROPOLITAN OPERAS
27 Short Plays

BY JOE PINTAURO

★

★

DRAMATISTS
PLAY SERVICE
INC.

For Nelson Algren

These plays were commissioned in 1985 by The Circle Repertory Company in New York City and were produced in The Lab, in three-evening cycles, under the title, RAPID FIRE. In 1995, for the first time ever, Dolphinback of Chicago produced the entire collection in marathon, day-long productions at the Theatre Building in Chicago under the title, AMERICAN DIVINE. Before that, the plays were produced in various constellations under titles such as: WILD BLUE (Glines, New York City, and Rhinocerous, San Francisco), MOVING TARGETS (Vineyard Theatre, New York City), METROPOLITAN OPERAS (Incline, Los Angeles), ON THE WING (The Barrow Group, New York City), SALVATION (The Gate, Nottinghill, London), THE SPIRIT (Traverse, Edinborough, Scotland).

TABLE OF CONTENTS

PART I

PART II

PART I

SEYMOUR IN THE
VERY HEART OF WINTER

CHARACTERS

BOB — an Italian-American chauffeur, good looking, street wise, in uniform. He's much younger than Vivienne, worshipfully in love with her.

VIVIENNE — pronounced Vivie-Yin by Bob. She assumes the superiority and physical grace of a royal public figure. Once a well-known actress, she has been out of work much too long. She is nearing or perhaps even past middle age. She is still unquestionably beautiful. She wears a full-length dinner dress and wrap, something Christmasy. The wrap, a regal cape of wool or fur from more prosperous days, hangs from her chair like a queen's robe.

WAITER — French. Formal. Impeccably dressed for a function in which he takes pride.

SETTING

A small, elegant restaurant in Greenwich Village, New York. We see only one table which, presumably, looks out upon the street. The table is beautifully set for Christmas Eve dinner — it holds a small centerpiece made of one red candle in its holder, surrounded by loose sprigs of holly. One salmon dinner is before Vivienne, untouched, and one is before Bob, almost totally consumed. An empty, floor-standing wine cooler is at hand. The wine bottle is on the table, all but empty.

SEYMOUR IN THE VERY HEART OF WINTER

As the play opens, we see the couple at table, Bob is eating hungrily, and Vivienne's just sitting, depressed, arms folded, looking out the window. The waiter stands nearby, patiently awaiting commands. His station is in rosy light which makes him, at times, almost completely indistinct. His contribution to the plot is minimal until the end and care must be taken not to mislead the audience by involving him in any way that raises unnecessary questions about him. The focus is on Vivienne and Bob.

BOB.   You haven't touched your food. That's a whole baby salmon.

VIVIENNE.   Tell him to give you a doggie bag. *(She sips her wine drowsily, looking out the window.)*

BOB.   This blows our food money for the week. *Vivienne?* You're ignoring me.

VIVIENNE.   I heard you.

BOB.   What I say?

VIVIENNE.   Something about ... the food.

BOB.   If I bore you have the guts to tell me.

VIVIENNE.   Will that change you?

BOB.   Bitch. I'm sorry.

VIVIENNE.   *(Sips.)* No. I am a bitch tonight. I am a bitch.

BOB.   If you're tired of me spit it out.

VIVIENNE.   I'll have dessert. Will that make you happy?

BOB.   I'm not your mommy, Vivienne.

VIVIENNE.   But I could be yours.

BOB.   Start in with our ages now, I'm walking outta here.

VIVIENNE.   Alright. Tell me.

BOB.   What?

VIVIENNE.   What wasn't I listening to? *(She closes her eyes as if listening to music.)*

BOB.   You act like you're alone here. I'm talkin' your eyes are on the waiter, you're out the window ... everything 'cept me. Now they're closed. Goodnight Vivienne. (*He waves sarcastically.*)

VIVIENNE.   Good wine relaxes me.

BOB.   Christmas Eve dinner is a big thing for Italians.

VIVIENNE.   I'll have dessert.

BOB.   This was your dessert, the wine. I'll take you to Rocco's for a cannoli.

VIVIENNE.   It's raining.

BOB.   I'll get the limo. You can ride in back.

VIVIENNE.   Oh let's stay.

BOB.   Turnin' down a ride in a limo? A famous actress like you?

VIVIENNE.   Don't hurt me ... don't ...

BOB.   You're *famous*. The waiter recognized you.

VIVIENNE.   I'm not famous. And I wouldn't be caught dead in that funeral car of yours if I could afford taxi cabs.

BOB.   There's always the subway.

VIVIENNE.   You know it scares me.

BOB.   Scared your friends'll catch you goin' for your unemployment checks?

VIVIENNE.   My friends know little about me.

BOB.   They know you're living with a chauffeur.

VIVIENNE.   Temporarily.

BOB.   It's over two years now, Viv.

VIVIENNE.   I don't want to go into this.

BOB.   I pay the rent. You sleep with me. What are we?

VIVIENNE.   I don't know. Go find a nice Italian girl and make her pregnant.

BOB.   Suppose I want you instead?

VIVIENNE.   Don't be ridiculous.

BOB.   Where will you go when the pregnant girl moves in?

VIVIENNE.   I'll kill myself.

BOB.   Thanks. (*Sarcastically.*) Merry Christmas. (*In the painful silence, Vivienne sips wine mournfully and reacts to people, outside the fourth wall, who are passing the restaurant window.*) You know you got like this last Christmas too. Vivienne? *(Reaches for her hand. She pulls her hand back, refusing to look anywhere but out the window, to the audience.)*

VIVIENNE.   Those manic Christmas shoppers. Don't they question it? Why? The summer ended only a couple weeks ago.

BOB.   You know what you look like in that dress with no jewelry and nothing except your lipstick? Viv? In this soft light?

VIVIENNE.   What.

BOB.   Like a painting, a Madonna.

VIVIENNE.   The shit's coming out of your ears.

BOB.   I'm not buying it, Vivienne. *(Vivienne's out the window, not listening.)*

VIVIENNE.   Maybe I won't kill myself. Look at them loaded down with presents, all excited. Boy are they askin' for it. *(Sips her wine.)* When I was a kid, I would've cut off my arm for a Christmas tree. I wanted to smell a big spruce in our living room and sleep under it on that rose-colored rug, looking up at the lights and the ornaments, having a real tree from the forest in our house ...

BOB.   Why didn't you?

VIVIENNE.   ... the smell of those trees in front of the stores at night, dark green giants all around as if you were suddenly lost in a pine forest ... I'd pick up a branch, hide it under my coat and sneak it to bed with me, holding it near my face, smelling the forest in the dark, pretending I was a way up north in a totally sunless country where people lived to be two hundred years old.

BOB.   *(Entranced.)* With no sun?

VIVIENNE.   No sun whatever. Just the Aurora Borealis and starshine and moons so bright you can read a newspaper. But there'd be no newspaper up there, no buses, trains, planes. No factories, no wars, no TV, just ... enormous giant pine trees and log cabins and fireplaces. There would be violence, but the holy kind. I mean rabbits and deer hanging dead in the pantry next to the mince pies, not the violence of the subways and streets, you get me? No guns except for the men to hunt for the women and children, and total trust, total trust ... because we'd all be cousins ... born and dying in each other's arms. Safe. And at night, during the blizzards, we'd all gather in big snow cellars lined with fur where we'd tell stories, all of us buried under the ice with our fur walls and fires, deep ... in the very heart of winter.

BOB.   God, can you story tell. *(Vivienne doesn't seem to hear him.)*

VIVIENNE.   That's why I wanted a Christmas tree, so I could sleep under it on the rug and dream of that place.

BOB.   You shoulda stood up to your father ...

VIVIENNE.   *(Proudly.)* I did. He lifted me onto his lap and took my hand and kissed the tips of my fingers. "We get something better," he said.

BOB.   And you believed him?

VIVIENNE.   Why not? He was right. We get the menorah, we get candles, latke parties, cakes and ... and then ...

BOB.   And then they died. Why didn't you go get a tree then?

VIVIENNE.   My aunts were orthodox. I was still a kid. I ...

BOB.   What about later with your husband?

VIVIENNE.   I didn't want a tree. Enough Christmas. It's the wine doing this to me. *(The Waiter puts the wine bottle in the bucket stand as if to remove it.)*

WAITER.   Coffee for Madame?

BOB.   We're invited somewhere for coffee.

WAITER.   Ze check?

BOB.   Just the check. *(Vivienne takes the bottle from the stand.)*

VIVIENNE.   Wait. There's wine left.

WAITER.   Oh, I am so soree.

BOB.   Vivienne, it's empty.

VIVIENNE.   There's more, see? *(She pours.)* See? *(Empties a tablespoonful.)*

WAITER.   Madame is right. *(Waiter takes bottle and stand and disappears.)*

BOB.   You ... ever hear from Seymour?

VIVIENNE.   He's teaching in Massachusetts.

BOB.   He writes to you?

VIVIENNE.   I hear through others.

BOB.   Him and his ... you know, boyfriend, still together?

VIVIENNE.   He's living with a student, a woman. I heard she's pregnant.

BOB.   Boy, does he change his mind.

VIVIENNE.   Please.

BOB.   It impressed me though about your divorce.

VIVIENNE.   What impressed you?

BOB.   The way he left you for a guy and still you said he was very sexy with you, that he took care of you, loved you.

VIVIENNE.   I said that?

BOB.   Ah-huh.

VIVIENNE.   I only got to know him as we were breaking up. I ...

BOB.   You, with a guy named Seymour. Kills me.

VIVIENNE.   What's funny about that?

BOB.   The name, Seymour.

VIVIENNE.   It's an English name.

BOB.   I just imagine some Jewish kid.

VIVIENNE.   Shut up!

BOB.   What.

VIVIENNE.   It's not even a Jewish name. It's French, from Maurice, meaning dark skinned, like a Moor ...

BOB.   Hey, okay ...

VIVIENNE.   ... Jane Seymour was fifth queen of Henry the Eighth ...

BOB.   *I'm with* ya.

VIVIENNE.   ... The Jews used Seymour to Anglicize the name Shimon, which was a royal name anyway. One of the twelve tribes of Israel ...

BOB.   Slow down.

VIVIENNE.   I'd give my right arm to be with him right now. I'd be sipping port and demitasse instead of staring at this shit. *(She throws her napkin on top of her dinner.)*

BOB.   That's twice you cut off your arm.

VIVIENNE.   Ignorant ...

BOB.   You cut off an arm for a Christmas tree ...

VIVIENNE.   I can't listen to you.

BOB.   The other arm for Seymour. You got no arms left, Viv. *(Beat.)* I'm sorry. Viv? Viv? How'd you meet your Seymour? I'm serious.

VIVIENNE.   He was the dramatics teacher in my high school.

BOB.   No. Wait. You married your high-school teacher?

VIVIENNE.   I used to clean house for my aunts to scrape up ticket money ... so I could go up to Mr. Elliot in the halls and say: *"I went to the theater last night."* I dyed my hair, my eyebrows. Let the hair grow under my arms. Dyed it.

BOB.   What color?

VIVIENNE.   Everything blue black.

BOB.   You're kiddin'.

VIVIENNE.   Brought spiked heels to school in a paper bag and wore sweaters with no bra. Went through Woolite like it was Coca Cola. I joined the dramatics society. He made me treasurer and gave the parts to everyone else. Even then I was smarter about the theater than he was. I hung out in those shady side streets, around the little ticket agencies, the stage doors, hoping to talk to a "star." I went up to "Mr. Eliot" in the halls: "I saw Julie Harris on Forty-fourth Street but I refused to ask for an autograph." He walked away. Seymour walked away if you tried to impress him, if you made the slightest boast. He feared the pain of inadequacy. The more you tried to impress him the more he punished you. And yet, I admired him for the shame he could make me feel. I actually believed he could cure me of my shame. I'd take the train home swearing I'd become a star whom he'd wanna marry some day and I succeeded, didn't I ... *(Her eyes are lost in the movie of her life playing out the window.)*

BOB.   He noticed your sweaters.

VIVIENNE.   No. Years later, I got a part in *Trojan Women* at Circle in the Square and who do I see in the audience one night?

BOB.   Woody Allen.

VIVIENNE.   Seymour with his pal, Bob Simonetti. On their

way to Yale to teach. Simonetti was in physics. He looked a little thin, a little depressed ...

BOB.   Seymour?

VIVIENNE.   He was balding ... his legs crossed and his arms folded like he was Arthur Miller. He had his, "I'm not available" look. But uh ... I grabbed his eye and made him smile. That's a hard thing to do from the stage, to make someone that depressed, who is in the audience, to smile. Everything I ever lost in my whole life was given back to me at that split second: my mother, my memories, the house.... Even my father was there in Seymour's little smile. Nothing ever came close to that thrill.

BOB.   Like a deep, sort of ... a burning feeling ... here?

VIVIENNE.   Burning, exactly, as if your lungs were suddenly on fire.

BOB.   I get that with you a lot. *(Again, Vivienne's so absorbed she can't hear.)*

VIVIENNE.   Right there I said to myself: How can I become pregnant by this man? How can I *trap* him? They went off to Yale and guess what I did?

BOB.   Followed him.

VIVIENNE.   I got a job in the bursar's office, went places with the two of them. When Simonetti transferred to M.I.T. Seymour asked me to move in with him.

BOB.   Just like that?

VIVIENNE.   Ten years we were married. One abortion that he insisted upon. I did a lot of acting. Met great people. Then. One night Seymour has to work. My girlfriends drag me to this jazz bar and he's supposed to be in rehearsal but he's sitting back in the shadows. I was shocked. He never went to those places. And who is he with?

BOB.   Simonetti's back?

VIVIENNE.   Simonetti has his arm around my husband, putting a drunken kiss on Seymour's lips. And Seymour gives him this ... this ... loving expression, which shocked me more than a cannon firing in my face. What a fool I was. I'm walking toward them, headless, blood dripping all over my dress, my hands out to both of them, like *"How nice to see you guys."* Seymour jumps up giving me a kiss, pulling up a chair, calling the waiter. *"No."* I said. *"Can't sit here.... Got to get back to my friends."* I'm walking away like a zombie, jazz playing, people laughing and screaming and I'm paranoid that everybody knew, all along, and maybe even that's why the girls dragged me there, to wake me up and I hated them ... I ...

BOB. Ever taste a Saint Joseph cake?

VIVIENNE. *(Dazed, exhausted.)* What? *(The Waiter approaches.)*

BOB. They're even better than canolis.

WAITER. *L'addition Monsieur?*

BOB. Just the check.

VIVIENNE. What's the rush? Let's have a glass of Port.

BOB. I wanna get out of here.

VIVIENNE. You're telling me I can't have a Port because you want a cannoli?

BOB. I'm tellin' you Rocco closes in ten minutes.

VIVIENNE. So? Who wants to sit under florescent lights and eat sugar? *(The Waiter disappears.)*

BOB. Dessert here's ten bucks. With coffee. That's another twenty five, I don't have it.

VIVIENNE. How dare you ... when I ... was ... speaking of ... *(She stands, snaps open her purse, searching intensely for a tissue.)* Get me outta here.

BOB. Sit down a minute. *(She sits. The Waiter arrives with a glass of Port and places it before Vivienne.)* What's that? I said the check.

WAITER. Compliments of the house for Madame.

BOB. Get it outta here. Take it.

WAITER. *Oui Monsieur. (He takes the port and disappears.)*

VIVIENNE. You goddamn rotten little sonofabitch.

BOB. No handouts. Okay? My parents didn't know the difference between Santa Claus and Uncle Sam, okay? You would never see them out there buyin' me a present. I was lucky there was a loaf of bread on the table. I offer you a ride in a limo. What do I have that I can *give* you? My ass is flat from ridin' in that thing you call a *funeral car* even though it saves you cab fares. Thirty bucks for a fish you didn't touch. The past was so great and today so shitty, you let a goddamn fish die on your plate for no reason except you're pissed off at Seymour and Christmas trees. I'm ignorant — I don't know how to talk — so what are you doin' with me? Your panty hose are drying on my door knobs, my shower curtain, all the chairs. My phone bill quadrupled, you owe me for the rent so I give you rubdowns and still you tell me it's temporary so you can get the hell away from me the minute the right job comes along, but it's Christmas Eve for cryin' out tears, and your big break isn't gonna come in the next twenty-four hours so please take your Christmas tree and your Seymour stories and file them under tough shit and let's get outta here and go get a cannoli and a cup of coffee where I could afford the fuckin' thing.

VIVIENNE.   Animal. Give me a handkerchief. *(Bob throws the large white napkin up to her, accidentally hitting her face. She catches it and throws it aside.)*

BOB.   I don't have a handkerchief. *(Vivienne goes back to her bag.)*

VIVIENNE.   You ... *(Waiter reappears, upset by what he perceives as Bob's insensitivity.)*

BOB.   Let's see ... dollar fifty on every ten ... *(The Waiter pulls out a neatly ironed handkerchief and offers it to Vivienne.)*

VIVIENNE.   Merci. *(She lifts her cape up from the chair and pretends to have accidentally dropped it. The Waiter rushes to catch it, missing it but he lifts it from the floor, whirls it as a bull fighter into position. She reaches back to receive it but his hands pass over hers, wrapping the cape around her. She only has to find the clasp which she does as he lifts her hair out from inside the wrap. She turns, caressing his hand with her cheek. He steps back from her, pleased with himself. His actions were within propriety, and yet it was all a brief, affectionate little dance.) Vous êtes très <u>très</u> gentile. (She gives the Waiter her hand. He bows deeply, kissing it. She puts on her dark glasses.)*

WAITER.   *Je vous en prie Madame. Joyeux Noel.*

BOB.   *Merci.*

WAITER. *Monsieur. (With a dirty look. The Waiter gathers the many bills on the table and exits. Bob presses close to Vivienne, taking her body against his, lovingly.)*

BOB. If you die before me, I'll never love another woman. Okay?

VIVIENNE. What good will that do me?

BOB. *(He turns away angrily.)* I may go before you.

VIVIENNE. No. Don't. *(She reaches up, touches his cheek, and leans her head against him.)*

BOB. It was the wine tonight, Viv.

VIVIENNE. No. The wine is innocent. Only the wine is innocent.

END

SWANS FLYING

CHARACTERS

NURSE ESTELLE — is over fifty.

BEN — a patient, is angelic, childlike, young.

EDDIE — Ben's visitor, is Ben's age; he's beautiful, graceful, and strong.

SETTING

A hospital bed floats in space near one white metal visitor's chair.

SWANS FLYING

It is dark, just before dawn in a hospital room. Ben, the patient, is half sitting in bed, staring, eyes fixed on a distance. He is a young poet. His Nurse sits in her own light in the dark room, on a white metal chair, legs crossed, alternately reading Time, Money, and New York magazines. On the floor, surrounding her, are enormous piles of old newspapers and magazines from back years.

The sounds Ben hears are to be heard by the audience. Nurse hears them too, but she denies them, as if only that which she reads in print has any reality for her. Ben certainly hears the underwater screams of the flounder being eaten by the seals, but it is not essential that we hear this particular sound. It is essential, however, that the sound of the swans flying be heard sharply and clearly by the audience. The sound of swans flying is often loud, like a chorus of bellows. The play opens with ocean sounds, pounding surf, etc., faintly heard, as if from afar. Yet, in the foreground, there are the trills of red-winged black birds.

BEN.   Water. *(Nurse looks up from her reading.)* I hear it. Oh yes. Estelle? Estelle, do you hear it?
NURSE.   Uh huh. *(She goes back to reading.)*
BEN.   Is the ocean close?
NURSE.   'Bout a mile away.
BEN.   What's the date, Estelle? *(Nurse looks at her watch.)*
NURSE.   April one.
BEN.   Oh yeah. Of course. I hear them, the red-winged blackbirds, bouncin' on the cattails. Do you hear screaming?
NURSE.   I certainly do not.

BEN.   Yes. Under the water ...

NURSE.   I certainly do not hear screaming under the water.

BEN.   The flounder are waking up, coming out of the mud ...

NURSE.   Uh huh.

BEN.   ... and the seals have found them, and they're eating them alive.... It hurts. Oh my God. How it hurts ... *(He abruptly stops talking, aware of a new sound.)* Estelle?

NURSE.   Uh huh?

BEN.   Do you hear swans?

NURSE.   I certainly do not hear swans.

BEN.   Shhhhhh. *(He sits up. Nurse ignores the rapid, whirring sounds of swans approaching. She continues her reading.)* There must be eight or ten of them, coming this way. Good luck Estelle. Good luck if swans fly over your head. And I think ... they will ... *(The sound becomes louder and the light brightens gradually with it.)* They will. Estelle.... Swans flying.... Swans flying. *(The sound peaks.)* Swans flying over our heads ... *(The whirring of swan wings has reached symphonic fullness here, then begins to fade gradually, as the swans pass on. The light stays bright however, like new morning light.)* I can sleep now. Please forgive me, Estelle, if I ... fall ... asleep. *(Soft, ocean sounds return. Ben drifts to sleep as Nurse whips through another magazine. Eddie enters so softly the Nurse doesn't notice. Eddie is dressed in a black coat and black gloves,. He carries spring flowers. The flowers must be fresh and real so that the audience catches their odor when they come into the room.)*

NURSE.   Oh. You startled me.

EDDIE.   Did he have a good night?

NURSE.   The usual.

EDDIE.   Did he ask for me?

NURSE.   Not a word.

EDDIE.   Take a break Estelle. *(Nurse pauses, as if reluctant to give up her post. She collects some magazines to take.)*

NURSE.   Today's paper?

EDDIE.   No thanks. *(Estelle exits. Eddie places the flowers alongside Ben, near his feet. Eddie pulls off his gloves, sits, leaning back*

24

patiently, stretching out his arm, lifting Ben's hand in his. Eddie does not take Nurse's chair, but his own, near Ben, at the side of his bed. He looks upon the sleeping face adoringly, watching him breathe, long and evenly. Strong breaths. He smiles, pleased. Lights fade to black-out.)

END

ROSEN'S SON

CHARACTERS

MR. ROSEN — is about sixty.
EDDIE — is forty.
HARRISON — is twenty-eight.

SETTING

An apartment foyer on the upper West Side of Manhattan, New York City.

ROSEN'S SON

Two men, one old enough to be the father of the other, are sitting on the floor of an apartment foyer. The older man is lying with his head in the lap of the younger, like a child who has been crying. There is quiet in the foyer, although we are aware that something awful has just happened, something that caused the men to collapse to the floor. The older man is still in his wet raincoat; his umbrella is on its side next to him, dripping on the floor tiles. The younger man, who apparently just answered his buzzer, obviously had been entertaining dinner guests. He is dressed handsomely for dinner. Perhaps some coats, hats, and umbrellas of guests are hanging in the small foyer. Doors to the foyer, imaginary or not, are closed, one supposedly locked.

MR. ROSEN. Forgive me, Eddie.

EDDIE. Shhhh.

MR. ROSEN. Do ya forgive me?

EDDIE. I think so.

MR. ROSEN. Where's the gun?

EDDIE. I've got it.

MR. ROSEN. Did I hurt you?

EDDIE. My lip's cut.

MR. ROSEN. I'm sorry.

EDDIE. Just take it easy. Relax.

MR. ROSEN. I've gone crazy. I miss my boy.

EDDIE. I miss him too, Mr. Rosen.

MR. ROSEN. So you get involved two months after he dies?

EDDIE. Your son was sick a long time.

MR. ROSEN. So you celebrate his death by moving a stranger in here to live with you?

EDDIE. He's no stranger.

MR. ROSEN. You call me "Mr. Rosen"?

EDDIE.   Alright. Ziggie. Take it easy.

MR. ROSEN.   Strangers' coats in my son's foyer.

EDDIE.   Just shut up.

HARRISON.   *(Off.)* Ed?

EDDIE.   Yeah?

HARRISON.   *(Off.)* Who buzzed?

EDDIE.   I'm taking care of it.

HARRISON.   *(Enters, speaking.)* Our guests are waiting…. Who is this man?

EDDIE.   Ben's father. *(To Mr. Rosen.)* This is Harrison.

HARRISON.   Mr. Rosen?

MR. ROSEN.   What else?

HARRISON.   My deepest sympathies … for your recent trouble. Would you care to join us? *(He indicates the dining room.)*

EDDIE.   No, Harrison …

MR. ROSEN.   I come here with a gun, he invites me to dinner?

HARRISON.   Does he have a gun?

EDDIE.   I took it from him.

MR. ROSEN.   Does he know who allows him to stand here in this foyer? My son. Because of his death you stand here. Is that true Eddie? I would vomit on that table in there.

HARRISON.   He's off his rocker …

EDDIE.   This is not him.

MR. ROSEN.   Young people, you have no heart, no memory, but wait. You'll get yours. Just let me outta this death oven.

EDDIE.   I'll call you later.

MR. ROSEN.   Call nothing. Which way out of this hell?

EDDIE.   *(Grabbing his coat, to Harrison.)* I've got to go with him.

HARRISON.   You're going?

EDDIE.   To see him home.

MR. ROSEN.   Are you crazy? For me what is home?

HARRISON.   Eddie, you can't just leave our dinner guests.

EDDIE.   Shut up, will you, Harrison?

HARRISON.   Are you aware of the tone you just used with me?

EDDIE.   *I said shut up.*

HARRISON. I'm calling the police. He's threatened us.

EDDIE. Do that, Harrison, and I'll leave you. I swear to Christ.

HARRISON. Did you say you'll leave me?

MR. ROSEN. Easy come, easy go.

HARRISON. *(Pointing at Mr. Rosen.)* You are trespassing, and it's criminal.

MR. ROSEN. Bite your tongue, cutie. Who do you think you are to get your bloomers in such an uproar over me? What do you see standing before you? An old man in a raincoat. One wife. One child. Both dead. Him I put in the diamond business. For you, bastard.

HARRISON. Does he mean me?

MR. ROSEN. Who do I mean, this umbrella? You start living with a man two months after his lover dies — are you the Blessed Virgin?

HARRISON. I knew Eddie a year.

MR. ROSEN. While my son was sick you fooled around, you pig in a fancy shirt.

EDDIE. He worked in our office.

HARRISON. You're wrong, Mr. Rosen.

MR. ROSEN. Drop in a hole the two of you. Young people. You replace other people like spark plugs. Half your age I said good-byes that would make you sweat blood. I cut the tattooed numbers off my wrist with a kitchen knife, then worried, without them, how would my sister find me. Don't worry. Your government brought the numbers back worse and you got them and no knife is sharp enough.... You. I tried to teach you, but only diamonds you learned, only money so you could marry Mister Bloomingdales here who tells me I trespass in my son's apartment? *Mazel tov.* Give me at least back my gun.

HARRISON. Don't give it to him.

EDDIE. Get inside, Harrison.

MR. ROSEN. Afraid to die so young, Mister Bloomingdales? My boy was not afraid. He smiled. Relax, Mister Bloomingdales, the gun was for my head not yours or his, though you are pigs enough to be slaughtered ...

EDDIE. Ziggie, please.

MR. ROSEN. Shame on people who eat with candles, not for God but to hide pimples and wrinkles. Young people who live together not for love but for sex, boff boff like pistons machines. You never get bored? *(To Harrison.)* What are you smiling at?

EDDIE. Harrison, go now. *(Harrison starts off.)*

MR. ROSEN. Not so fast, cutie. You want to make a deal? You change places?

HARRISON. With who?

MR. ROSEN. My boy?

HARRISON. Oh, Eddie.

MR. ROSEN. You crawl into his grave and send my son home to his father?

HARRISON. I'm so sorry for you, Mr. Rosen ...

EDDIE. Harrison's a good person.

MR. ROSEN. Young people living in a magazine. Did you show him a picture of my boy? *(Mr. Rosen takes a photo out of his wallet.)*

EDDIE. Jesus!

HARRISON. I'm not afraid. I'd like to see him.

MR. ROSEN. *(Showing him the photo.)* Look at a beautiful face. Eh?

HARRISON. Very nice.

MR. ROSEN. You ... *(To Eddie.)* What's his name?

EDDIE and HARRISON. Harrison.

MR. ROSEN. *(To Eddie.) Goyisha? (Eddie nods yes.)* Harrison. Where do they get these names?

HARRISON. It's a family name.

MR. ROSEN. Your nose is a fortune cookie next to my son. I'm serious.

EDDIE. Okay, Ziggie, let's call it quits.

MR. ROSEN. A basketball is your neck. My way of speaking. You play an instrument?

HARRISON. I've always regretted not ...

MR. ROSEN. The flute, my son ... Avery Fisher Hall. Clippings to drown in.

HARRISON. He's extraordinary. He's beautiful. *(Handing back the photo.)* Eddie, our guests are waiting.

MR. ROSEN. I came here to splash my brains over your table. That's what the gun was for, to put out your candles with my blood.

HARRISON. Please.

MR. ROSEN. But I changed my mind. In the river throw the gun. Me, I'll do like the elephants: Go to Miami. The sun will polish my bones. For a little fee, a lawyer will send you my tusks. They'll go nice here, either side of your door. Speaking of doors, kindly point the way a person gets out of here.

HARRISON. May I be excused please?

MR. ROSEN. Leave. *Mazel tov. (Harrison exits. Mr. Rosen stares long at Eddie.)* You forgot the summers at the lake, the canoe, the three of us? The dinners? The holidays, birthdays? I had to accept you, didn't I? I had to swallow it. And I did. And you just forgot those days?

EDDIE. I didn't forget any of it.

MR. ROSEN. Were we really together then?

EDDIE. I thought we were.

MR. ROSEN. I thought so, too. I thought so. *(Eddie puts on his coat.)* Where you goin'?

EDDIE. To help you get a taxi.

MR. ROSEN. No taxi.

EDDIE. Then I'll call you later to see you got home safe.

MR. ROSEN. Never dare call me again in your life. You're nothing to me.

EDDIE. Don't say that.

MR. ROSEN. Liar. You want I should disappear so bad.

EDDIE. No.

MR. ROSEN. Look at his face. Such a liar. After this minute, never, never again will you see this face of your "Mr. Rosen." But before I go I want you should tell me a truth, so perfect as you never before spoke the truth to anyone in your life, and I'll give you the freedom of a thousand doves set loose on the mountain tops.

EDDIE. Ask me.

MR. ROSEN.   Do you love that one in there? The truth before God.

EDDIE.   I'm trying to love him. I'm the kind of man who has to have somebody ... I'm trying very hard. *(Mr. Rosen moves in on Eddie, beating him down with questions.)*

MR. ROSEN.   Does he take care of you like—?

EDDIE.   *(Overlap.)* He's different ...

MR. ROSEN.   Like my boy used to? Remember —

EDDIE.   *(Overlap.)* Different.

MR. ROSEN.   Like you were God on Earth?

EDDIE.   No ... *(Mr. Rosen hammers at Eddie till he breaks.)*

MR. ROSEN.   Does he laugh with those same funny eyes ...

EDDIE.   Of course not.

MR. ROSEN.   Bake bread like he used to?

EDDIE.   No. *(Losing it.)*

MR. ROSEN.   Play the flute on Sunday while you read the paper?

EDDIE.   No. No.

MR. ROSEN.   The truth before God.

EDDIE.   *(Cries, screams, pounds Mr. Rosen's chest.) It'll never be the same for me again. Never.*

MR. ROSEN.   This is true?

EDDIE.   What do you think? *(Eddie sinks till he is on the floor at Mr. Rosen's feet, weeping.)* You bastard, you awful man.

MR. ROSEN.   Good you cry. Now I'm happy. Goodbye, Eddie. Don't follow me. Don't call me. God bless you. You were my son. Really. You were. My other son. *(Mr. Rosen exits, lights fade on Eddie.)*

END

BENJAMIN FALLING

BENJAMIN FALLING

*Benjamin has just stepped out the door of a plane at fif-
teen thousand feet. He is falling in space, suspended in air
like Christ on the cross.*

BENJAMIN. I said to Eddie, my inhibitors aren't working so
how much do we have in the bank? Sixty thousand? I said,
Eddie, I don't wanna do it like the guy in *Martin Eden,* that
book by Jack London? Take a steamer to the middle of the
ocean and then slip out a port hole and ... just deal with it,
whatever ... sharks, fatigue, sucking up water ... I mean, that
... that could lead to like the big ass of this big ship is going
away from you and you're weaving in the turbulence and then
what? You taste the water. It's salty but will this kill you? No
way. You could be stuck out there saying what the fuck did I
do this for? Who wrote *Brooklyn Bridge,* the poet, what's his
name...? Oh you know him. No, not Gerard Manly Hopkins
that hound of heaven shit.... You know the guy. He booked
a ride on a cruise ship with some woman down near Mexico
and just slipped over the side while she waited for him at dinner, dressed in this chiffon thing and she never saw him
again. Fabulous. Just think of your friends imagining you in
all that water and space, alone. Just your head on the hori-
zon, the sky and Bhudda. You have taken your life into your
own hands, literally diving off this culture mentality, off Money
Magazine off People magazine, off Hollywood, television...,
zing! into pure flat nature, into fucking mother nature. So
there you are in the water, oceanic, infinite. You're dog pad-
dling two hours and you're saying, so swallow some water already. But a man just can't drown by ... "drinking," not even
at a bar. You could buy a case of Evian and even that won't
do it because you'll just piss all night. No. It's got to go into
the lungs. It's got to stop the oxygen, stop the heart. You can't
do it. So I said to Eddie, how much do we have in the bank.
Why? Because the idea of water appeals to me, the ocean ap-

peals to me but I don't want to try it like from the QE-2. *(The sound of a single engine plane.)*

We'll buy this airplane and one case of Dom Perignon. Now we own the plane, okay? We fill it with gas ... small plane. Nothing that could reach England, I mean ... like something that could go from New York to ... around Bermuda. Screw the North Atlantic. Too gray. Too cold. I need pool temperature, an ocean the color of cough drops: aquamarine, ultramarine. Now, as the fuel gage gets lower and lower so does the Dom Peringnon and we run out of gas and champagne at the exact same moment. Suddenly, the propeller stops. Put. Put ... butta-put butta ... put. Put. And then ... *(The sound of whistling air.)*

... silence, except for our wings cutting the air. We're dropping out of the noise of the whole fucking century, the whole industrial revolution, the whole fucking combustion era. All that Time Warner, TBS noise, all that Washington noise, that Swartznagger noise, all that CBS-Westinghouse jingle-jangle, Eddie, kiss this whole rinky-dink, contraption ridden, loud, toxic, stripped, fuming, globally heated planet, goodbye from fifteen thousand feet up. Eddie, before we jump, I want to be naked. You ever read that James Dickey poem, where the stewardess gets sucked out of a plane and she finds herself up here, falling. Her life is over in eleven minutes, eleven minutes is a long time till you hit the ground, so she dances in the air, takes off her clothes, her bra, everything and has a ball. Open the door, Eddie. C'mon Sweetie, hold my hand and let's be gone with the wind and free-fall to that school of dolphins below and our bodies will hit, splat! and explode and all those pretty tropical fish will feast on our bodies and all that red meat will make their colors brighter. *What did you just say?* I'll make them ... sick? You always get awkward at the most sensitive times. What good are you? I'm here in Saint Vincent's and the only ascendant thing you give me is a mylar get-well balloon? Why *shouldn't* I expect more? My inhibitors aren't working. I don't know why. Become a doctor. Go into research. Picket the Center for Disease Control. Pray. Cry. Run through the streets and wake people up. Help me you fucking clown. *(Sounds of falling and of air whistling stop abruptly.)*

I had a dream. I just realized. I was in bed with Addison DeWitt, the critic in *All About Eve*. Who played him? George Sanders. I'm in the Caribbean with George and he dies on me but somehow he shows up the next day at New York magazine as Gail Sondergaard disguised as John Simon. No you couldn't remember Gail. I don't know how I do. God help me, this medication is so perverse. Eddie, you gotta help me. I am trapped in my youth with no way out. Not even the American Association of Retired People can help me. I'm too young for Medicare and too young to die. It's a big dilemma, having a mortal disease at my age. It's like ... are you asking me to drink this whole ocean? You've got to get it into your lungs and that is something I have an involuntary response to. Does anybody know how a young person gets out? I'm on fire and there's no fire escape. Eddie? Focus on me. I'm talking. Only love ... *(Shock!)* Whattaya mean what am I saying? Don't make fun of me. It's only you I got to pass through. Well it's *love*, what the fuck do you want me to call it? Alright. I'll stop. It's a cliché you're right. It's a soap opera. I got it. But remember Eddie. Denial is not a river in Egypt. Do I have to hear this? I know it's hard for you. What do you think it is for me? WaduIwanya to say? Say you'll jump with me. That was *not* wishing you dead. Okay I'm sorry. *Did you hear me say I'm sorry?* Just take care of the apartment, take care of the cat. Yes, yes. It's premature. I'm premature. The world is premature. Don't come near me. No kiss today. Please. Huh — whut? No. It couldn't've been Robert Frost Eddie. Robert wrote about Vermont. Wallace Stevens? Never. He lived in the Waldorf and wrote about Key West. It was Hart Crane. Hart Crane wrote *The Brooklyn Bridge*. God, I remembered! Am I happy now? Thrilled. I remembered something and you never even knew it to begin with. Memory is not that painful. You should try it. You might even remember me. *(Instant blackout, so fast the actor lingers in the mind's eye for a few seconds.)*

END

TWO ECLAIRS

CHARACTERS

MAUD — over twenty.

MARK — over twenty.

BETH — eighteen or under.

SETTING

Loft or apartment. Mark has taken up sculpting huge flight forms, as if his unconscious is working on some sort of escape plan. Absurdly large, the wing is perhaps several times larger than Mark himself and is all too obviously present on stage. His wing is a delicate skeleton. It may resemble a gigantic balsa plane model. Or, it may be a more fantastic wing form.

TWO ECLAIRS

Mark is fitting large sheets of foil or colorful paper to the wing as Maud enters, dressed in executive clothes, carrying groceries and her attaché case and keys from the door she just opened.

MARK. Hi. *(Maud plops down case and places shopping bag on the table.)*

MAUD. Hey, you've gotten far with that thing. I'm impressed. *(Kisses Mark, who is engrossed in work on the model. She hangs up her jacket and starts removing groceries from the shopping bag.)* I did something wonderful today. You'll be proud of me. Mark?

MARK. You sold the Twin Towers.

MAUD. Much better.

MARK. Really? Much better? Makes an airplane wing look silly no doubt.

MAUD. There's nothing creative about real estate, but it'll pay the rent until you … *(Whoops.)*

MARK. Get a job?

MAUD. Did I say get a job? I consider this wing your job.

MARK. You do, eh?

MAUD. It'll do till the muses stop picketing the building.

MARK. Maybe I *should* get a job. *(She imposes herself into his arms.)*

MAUD. You're an artist. It's like being a little God.

MARK. You'll take any old shit from me.

MAUD. Tell me you love me.

MARK. What's the wonderful thing?

MAUD. Did I tell you I've had dreams of flying?

MARK. In airplanes?

MAUD. No. *(Opening arms.)* In the nude. I'm asleep, and suddenly air's blowing on me so I open my eyes expecting to see the ceiling fan and instead I'm two thousand feet *up* looking down at a bridge. The East River's down there, and I'm headed toward the Atlantic. *(Simulating flying.)* And suddenly....Why? Am I? Not faaaalling? Oh-ma-god, how do I stay *up?* Got to will myself to be *up.* Gotta fly or I'll fall. And I squeeze every ounce of *willpower-ohmagod*-if I weaken I crash. So I throw my *soul* and *body* into staying *up.* Aaaaand I veeeer to the left ... I'm goin' toward Queens. Oh-ma-god, I'm *flying* over Queens. There's Aqueduct Race Track, Jamaica Bay, and suddenly, oh.... I'm over the *oooocean* and it's gloooorious, so I dive down. *(Confidence.)* I become acrobatic. I can do it. I swoop down and skim the water. I'm ... spray in my face, I'm ... a speedboat kissing the water so I shoot up straight like a rocket, five, ten thousand feet *up* through the hole in the ozone, past the sun, till I'm up with a whole new bunch of stars, in a totally new nighttime ...

MARK. Was that the wonderful thing? The dream?

MAUD. No. But that dream gave me the confidence to *do* the wonderful thing. To start, I bought two eclairs for our dessert, and ...

MARK. That's wonderful?

MAUD. No. Okay. What's wonderful is that ... Beth is gone. We have this entire place to ourselves. That's wonderful.

MARK. Gone? I mean ...

MAUD. I said, Beth, you're my sister, Mark and I love you, but when we said a few days, we didn't mean eight months ... and you've got to get out for your own sake more than ours, that it's all workspace up here, one bedroom, one bathroom, and it's not healthy to sleep on a couch and share a bathroom with a married couple, and it's not easy for you to work with my kid sister around all day.

MARK. She's out most of the time.

MAUD. Well, I was trying to make a good case out of it.

MARK. But she never bothers me.

MAUD. But eight months, she's gotta go. You're the one who said so. Why'd I do this?

MARK. Okay, okay. When is she leaving?

MAUD. Okay. This is what will surprise you. I said tomorrow.

MARK. Good for you.

MAUD. It was like flying, once I got started it all just came out of me and when she asked ..."When?" it flew out of my mouth like Vaseline. *(Mark is about to explode. He can't fake it.)*

MARK. Where the hell is a kid her age gonna go on such short notice?

MAUD. Huh?

MARK. She's quiet, she just ... amazes me how she's so invisible here. She must change her clothes in the damn closet.

MAUD. Markie ...

MARK. I've never *once* had to wait for the bathroom. I've had to wait for *you* ...

MAUD. She's my mother's problem.

MARK. I don't give a good god damn about your shit-face mother ...

MAUD. Huh?

MARK. Your mother's the problem here.... You're driving me crazy I ... am going crazy very well all by myself here twenty-four hours a goddamn day. I can't finish this thing. What in the damn. Dang.... Goddamn.... Sonofabitch ... *(He tears the foil or paper off his wing, punching it into balls.)* am I supposed to *do* here all day...?

MAUD. Mark...?

MARK. ... Wait to die? So I'm back to being alone all day. The woman doesn't even make noise when she runs the fucking water...

MAUD. I can't believe this.

MARK. She's like an *angel* around here. Oh God.

MAUD. *(Stunned.)* She's a very good kid

MARK. Go away. Go outside. Go for a walk. Please.... Forgive me. *(Maud just stares at her husband, confused by his reaction. She stiffly walks to a spot on stage where she takes a moment to think.)* I'm not saying what you did was mean ... or wrong. The girl has to go sometime. I know that as well as you do, but it's putting it in my face that way.

MAUD. You had sex with her. You had sex with my sister.

MARK. Oh for heaven's sake, no.

MAUD. You're lying.

MARK. ... Jesus.

MAUD. *(She's falling as in her dream now.)* God help me.

MARK. Take it easy. This is like lightning.

MAUD. I ... don't know ... I ... I don't know how I'm going to ... to live.

MARK. Oh please.

MAUD. I'm afraid to be all alone. Oh God, I'm falling, Mark. Going down ... through the clouds.

MARK. Stop your catastrophic thinking. C'mere. *(He becomes physically affectionate, caring.)*

MAUD. Losing my breath.

MARK. Breathe. *(She's torn between breaking away from his touch and needing him to physically balance her.)*

MAUD. Gonna die in a minute, Mark. I'm gonna ...

MARK. You're just feeling very strong feelings. They won't kill you. Look at me.

MAUD. Do you love her?

MARK. Don't torture yourself.

MAUD. Tell me and get it over with.

MARK. She loves me.

MAUD. So we are going to break up you and me?

MARK. C'mon ...

MAUD. Don't play with me, if you're gonna push a knife into me stab me all at once all the way, are we gonna break up?

MARK. We're discussing it.

MAUD. Who? You and she?

MARK. Right.

MAUD. Discussing your relationship with me?

MARK. *All* our relationships. *(Maud makes a dash for the closet. Pulls out suitcase. Madly starts packing.)*

MAUD. Gotta go. Gotta ... get outta here. *(Mark tries to stop her, to hold her.)*

MARK. Now please, don't panic.

MAUD. No. No. Don't touch me.

MARK.   People get through these things. Our friends have all been through this ...

MAUD.   Not me.

MARK.   What?

MAUD.   Not with my family.

MARK.   What are you saying?

MAUD.   They've ... they've finally killed me, finally killed me! Keep the place.

MARK.   Huh? You're being irrational ...

MAUD.   I can't talk straight. Don't care. *(She grabs the dish liquid and the bakery box.)*

MARK.   You can't just leave in a minute. *(Key sound in door.)*

MAUD.   What's that?

MARK.   She's here. Go in the bedroom.

BETH.   *(Enters.)* Hi. *(Kisses Mark, walks over to kiss Maud.)* Where are you going?

MAUD.   Into the bedroom.

BETH.   With dish liquid?

MAUD.   Oh. Here. *(Maud's coordination is so confounded that she hands Beth the bakery box instead of the dish liquid.)*

BETH.   What is it?

MAUD.   Oh. Have one. *(Exits, still clutching the dish liquid.)*

BETH.   Did you talk to her?

MARK.   Yeah. *(Beth opens the bakery box and pulls out an eclair, sits, and starts eating it. She giggles with a mouthful, offering the other eclair in its box to Mark. Mark stares, outraged. Beth's smiles evolve quickly to a bland sadness and the mood goes straight to Hell. As Mark starts tearing the wing apart, lights go down.)*

END

BIRDS IN CHURCH

CHARACTERS

TIM — a priest
ROB — a priest

SETTING

A cathedral.

BIRDS IN CHURCH

Tim and Rob are parish priests. They wear cassocks with the sleeves rolled up and white collars removed, opened at the top casually. Rob is in the audience with a collection basket. Tim stands onstage.

ROB. Are you sure the church is empty?

TIM. I just locked the doors.

ROB. The sacristy door is open.

TIM. Well you close it.

ROB. I haven't finished looking back here yet. Will you close the fashtinga sacristy door?

TIM. No. I think that this all has got to stop.

ROB. Shut up. Don't move. Don't move. *(He starts towards him.)*

TIM. Where is it?

ROB. Behind you.

TIM. Oh, I hate this.

ROB. What colors! Blue and and ... I guess lavender with black and white zebra stripes on its head.

TIM. You're trying to scare me.

ROB. No. It's gorgeous.

TIM. Well, you'll kill it with that basket. It's not a flying ten-dollar bill.

ROB. Now it's gone.

TIM. You are putting me on ...

ROB. No.

TIM. ... so you can babble at the table and make a fool of me.

ROB. That was the closest we came to it.

TIM. Now blame me.

ROB. You moved.

TIM.   Oh, there's no bird. I'm going to turn off the church lights.

ROB.   You think I'm lying?

TIM.   Give me that thing. After three days I would have seen a zebra striped lavender blue-green. *(He freezes, stunned.)* Oh. Sweet. Lord. It's gorgeous.

ROB.   Where ...

TIM.   It's yellow.

ROB.   It is not yellow.

TIM.   ... with iridescent ... gold and orange?

ROB.   It's all blue with purple ... and ...

TIM.   Are you mad? Look. *(Rob sees and grabs Tim.)*

ROB.   Oh, my God. There must be two of them.

TIM.   It's coming at us.

ROB.   Gimme that. *(The collection basket.)*

TIM.   Outta the way. It's mine. *(As in baseball.)*

ROB.   To the left. *(Both men duck as if dive-bombed.)*

TIM.   Where'd it go?

ROB.   Give me that. *(He takes the basket from Tim.)* Close the sacristy door. *(Tim makes for the rear of the theatre.)*

TIM.   I'm opening every door in this church, then I'm dragging you into the rectory.

ROB.   What? You saw the bird.

TIM.   That's right and it's going to fly out the way it flew in, both of them.

ROB.   It's freezing out. How are tropical birds going to survive a New York winter?

TIM.   Better than us swinging a collection basket at them. They haven't touched the corn muffin or the water you left.

ROB.   I told you to buy bird seed.

TIM.   If you'd have taken the choir, I'd have gone for the bird seed.

ROB.   We'd be killing these birds if we open those doors.

TIM.   Well, they flew in here, Robbie.

ROB.   Do you really believe they flew in here? Across Sixth Avenue? Across traffic? Through one of these rarely opened silly little church doors?

TIM. Now, Robbie, this isn't a miracle.

ROB. How do you know?

TIM. I'm getting nauseous.

ROB. The birds are those paradise types ...

TIM. Paradise types?

ROB. From a tropical, natural paradise.

TIM. They're probably parakeets from a swampy bog in Florida or the pet department of Lamston's across the street.

ROB. Or from somewhere beyond ... beyond our ...

TIM. Ooop! It's coming straight at us.

ROB. From where?

TIM. Get down! *(They crouch, shut their eyes, then rise.)*

ROB. There was nothing that time.

TIM. Didn't you see it?

ROB. I saw nothing.

TIM. You're lying.

ROB. Where're you going?

TIM. To open the doors.

ROB. No. One more day.

TIM. There are four Masses tomorrow. Once that organ starts these birds will have a heart attack, even if they do come from *'beyond.'*

ROB. Don't pull that sarcasm on me now ...

TIM. It's not as if it were a dove or a white pigeon, for heaven's sake.

ROB. Why couldn't the Holy Spirit be a bird of many colors?

TIM. Because these birds are sensual ...

ROB. Sensual?

TIM. Vivid, ostentatious. A dove or a pigeon would survive a winter in New York. It wouldn't have to hide in here.

ROB. That's precisely it. These birds came to this church vibrant, alive, but so delicate, so rare. They'll die of starvation or if they escape, they'll freeze to death. It's really more like a bird from Heaven than a dove.

TIM. You're talking metaphorically, I hope.

ROB. Well, yes.

TIM. Since when is God so delicate?

ROB. God is delicate. Or else He'd still be among us.

TIM. What did you say?

ROB. Did I say that?

TIM. Give me that basket and get into the rectory.

ROB. No. *(Sudden defense-collapse.)*

TIM. Give it to me.

ROB. You.... Get the hell away from me. You're a total disappointment.

TIM. *(Carefully, awed.)* Robbie ... I didn't mean ...

ROB. This is not a joke. *(He sits, falling into an altar chair.)*

TIM. What's upsetting you like this? Surely not these little birds?

ROB. Oh, I'm sick of you all.

TIM. You're turning the birds into too much.

ROB. If they die, I'll never set foot into this place again. *(He looks up and around then, losing control a little, he comes to midstage, picks up the bowl of water in one hand and the bowl of crumbled muffin in the other, falls down on his knees, opens wide his arms, and offers the food upward, shouting angrily.)* Come down.

TIM. Shhhh Robbie.

ROB. *Come down you damned birds and eat and drink and live.*

TIM. They won't eat a crumbled corn muffin. That was stupid ...

ROB. Why didn't you buy the seed?

TIM. Tomorrow. I will ...

ROB. It'll be too late. No food or water, they'll die of terror.

TIM. Not if they're from beyond. *(Dirty look from Rob.)*

ROB. You think God can't die of terror?

TIM. What...?

ROB. Suppose these birds are ...

TIM. The birds are what?

ROB. ... *of* God.

TIM. That's a little better.

ROB. Wait. *(Walks down the pew.)* What is that? Who left that here? *(Rob lifts cage, hidden till now, in which there is a bag of parakeet seed and a booklet. Tim pulls out the booklet.)*

TIM. How long has this been here?

ROB. Hartz Mountain parakeet seed and what's that booklet?

TIM. *How to Breed Budgies?*

ROB. Read the note. *(Tim tears open a pink letter.)*

TIM. "We are Chee-Chee and Blue Belle."

ROB. Chee-Chee and Blue Belle?

TIM. "... Our Mistress has left New York to join her boyfriend in Vermont. We love to fly and we are having a ball here in Saint Joe's. Fill the dishes in our cage then throw some seed in the air. The noise of seed hitting the floor makes us hungry and we go into our cage. If you adopt us, cover the cage on the way home as we detest winter. No cats, please." Where are you taking that cage?

ROB. I'm putting it right on the altar.

TIM. Robbie.

ROB. Just overnight and don't tell me it's sacrilegious. *(He places the cage upon the altar and starts filling the feeders inside it. He then positions the cage door so that it is obviously open.)*

TIM. Robbie, this note is not from God.

ROB. How do you know?

TIM. God does not have a boyfriend in Vermont.

ROB. Don't be so dogmatic.

TIM. That cage must be out of here before the first Mass.

ROB. It will be. Come here. Grab a handful. *(Tim and Rob both hold one fistful of seed.)* Now throw. *(Facing the middle aisle, they throw the seed in unison. Rob looks up expectantly; Tim looks at Rob worriedly.)*

TIM. C'mon. Let's get some sleep. Robbie?

ROB. Do you think they'll go in?

TIM. Not while we're watching. *(He pulls Rob. They exit, church lights start going out, but one light remains, illuminating the altar and the cage with its open door. Slow fade to blackout.)*

END

REX

CHARACTERS

ERIC — is a famous painter. His white trousers and shoes are colorfully splattered. For dinner he is wearing a tuxedo jacket. His hair is wet and combed neatly.

JENN — is dressed in expensive Soho chic. She's young, beautiful, spoiled. They are extremely wealthy.

SETTING

Dining room in an apartment in Soho, in New York City. The table is exquisitely set for two. Candles are lit, and a female voice singing an operatic aria is heard over perfect speakers.

REX

Eric is eating pumpkin seeds and munching as he speaks.

ERIC. Spend the day at the gym?

JENN. I drove out to the country.

ERIC. How was the house?

JENN. Survived the winter.

ERIC. Plumber turn the water on?

JENN. Yeah. Rosaria was cleaning when I left.

ERIC. Why didn't you stay?

JENN. I had to make it back.

ERIC. Georgette Klinger?

JENN. No.

ERIC. Tai chi?

JENN. No.

ERIC. You went to the Zen center.

JENN. I ... I wanted to chat with the new priest.

ERIC. The cute young priest.

JENN. I had a minor moral question.

ERIC. Cut the crap.

JENN. It had to do with the food on this table.

ERIC. Had enough macro? *(Lifting the plate, smelling.)* Tofu with scallions? What's the sauce?

JENN. Sesame oil.

ERIC. Out of a bottle.

JENN. I didn't say I slaved over it.

ERIC. And this ... *(Lifts plate.)* Is what? *(Shock. Drops plate, moves his chair back in horror.)* God, Jenn. What is that?

JENN. Okay just hear me out.

ERIC. It's some sort of meat.

JENN. Eric, we must eat flesh tonight.

ERIC. Eat flesh? Have you gone crazy?

JENN. It's organic.

ERIC. Of course it's organic. It's flesh.

JENN. I mean no steroids or antibiotics.

ERIC. Who guaranteed you that?

JENN. Eric, this bird is from the wild.

ERIC. Bird? It looks like tuna fish salad with a chicken leg stuck in the middle.

JENN. I had to shred the creature.

ERIC. Why didn't you shred the leg?

JENN. The leg was intact, so I left it ... I feel ill.

ERIC. I'm not eating this fucking thing.

JENN. We've got to. I killed it.

ERIC. You ... what? You ...

JENN. I ran over it with the Mercedes.

ERIC. A chicken?

JENN. No. A pheasant.

ERIC. Call our nutritionist.

JENN. It's a higher matter than that.

ERIC. Call your therapist.

JENN. For a massage?

ERIC. Not your massage therapist, your analyst for God's sake.

JENN. She'd only want to know what we think about it. The Zen priest said if we take it into our own bodies, it'll re-enter the life stream.

ERIC. It'll turn to shit is all.

JENN. Oh, fuck you.

ERIC. Nothing in Buddhism says you have to eat it because you killed it. Murderers would have to eat their victims. This is obscene.

JENN. Are you classifying me with ...

ERIC. You didn't murder it, I didn't say you murdered it. But you did kill it.

JENN. I killed it.

ERIC. You said you killed it. Okay, you ran over it ... and as a result.... What am I saying? You killed it.

JENN. I did not murder this bird.

ERIC. I said you only killed it.

JENN. I tried to save the fucking thing.

ERIC. Okay, take it easy.

JENN. It was flopping around in the road, limping, dizzy.

ERIC. Dear God.

JENN. I lifted it by its wing and threw it into the back seat and nearly killed myself driving to the vet.

ERIC. You went to the veterinarian with this...? *(He lifts the dish.)*

JENN. He worked on it for an hour.

ERIC. He worked on this?

JENN. It died in his hands.

ERIC. This is an expensive little dish.

JENN. He didn't charge, but it cost sixty bucks for the container ...

ERIC. What container? *(Jenn pulls up a small casket from one of the chairs. He recoils.)* That's a ... little casket.

JENN. The whole thing is made of pressed oatmeal so it's biodegradable ...

ERIC. Get that fucking thing off my dinner table.

JENN. They were going to incinerate it.

ERIC. Isn't that what you did anyway?

JENN. I roasted it.

ERIC. Oh my God she's gone over the falls. Should we eat every mosquito we slam?

JENN. You rotten ...

ERIC. We'd gag on the cockroaches we put away in our lifetimes, you and I.

JENN. What do you want me to do you sonofabitch?

ERIC. Throw the fucking bird in the garbage.

JENN. That's not right.

ERIC. Then eat the goddamn disgusting thing.

JENN. Okay. You take a bite and I'll take a bite and we'll put the rest in here and forget the whole thing.

ERIC. A casket made of oatmeal?

JENN. ... just a pet casket.

ERIC. A pet ...

JENN.   It decomposes and makes the animal one with the earth.

ERIC.   It'd be one with the earth if you'd've left it in the road.

JENN.   The crows would have picked at it.

ERIC.   So caw, caw. We're two giant crows at a dinner table in Soho, picking at a bird that was run over by a Mercedes Benz in East Hampton. You're getting a part-time job.

JENN.   You're freaking me.

ERIC.   I'm *freaked!* Get that casket off my dinner table.

JENN.   Listen to me. I don't know how things got this far, okay? But just end it and put the thing in the oatmeal thing and bury it.

ERIC.   Who bury it? Me bury it? Should we bury our toenail clippings? The hair we cut? In teeny weeny oatmeal caskets? I'm going to call Ruth's emergency number. *(He makes as if to exit.)*

JENN.   Call for yourself, wimpella.

ERIC.   Wimpella? Wiiiimpellaaaah?

JENN.   Just taste it. I said taste the goddamn thing and stop being such a troublemaker.

ERIC.   *(Tastes.)* What can I tell you? It's not bad.

JENN.   Are you kidding?

ERIC.   You marinated it.

JENN.   I just used olive oil, ginger, lemon, pepper ...

ERIC.   *(Eating more.)* Oh, Jenn, remember duck?

JENN.   Duck. My God.

ERIC.   Lamb chops. Bacon? *(They clutch hands. In unison:)*

JENN and ERIC.   Ham Hawaiian?

JENN.   Shut my mouth. *(But Eric bites into something hard and nearly cracks a tooth.)* Oh oh. *(He takes it out of his mouth, drops it on the dish. It clinks like a chunk of lead.)* Don't tell me your tooth...?

ERIC.   *(He lifts it.)* Asphalt. You eat.

JENN.   Oh. *(She tastes it. Makes a face.)*

ERIC.   What ...

JENN.   Meat. Disgusting.

ERIC.   Now swallow. Swallow.

JENN. Oh. There. I did it. I feel dizzy.

ERIC. Now why don't I go down to the dumpster and heave this little heap. No ceremony ...

JENN. First put it in the ... that.

ERIC. *(Eric lifts it, cradled in tinfoil.)* Tinfoil doesn't decompose, darling.

JENN. So what the fuck am I to do? Here ... *(She pulls the tinfoil out from under the bird as it drops into the casket, rolls the foil into a ball, and uncovers a silver dish.)*

ERIC. What's that?

JENN. The bones. *(She dumps the bones into the oatmeal casket.)* Now put on the lid. *(Eric does.)* God thank you. Now, I have lemon tarts for desert.

ERIC. No lemon tarts. Tonight we fast.

JENN. Thanks for understanding this silliness.

ERIC. Can you handle the truth darling?

JENN. What?

ERIC. I understand none of this. *(He throws on a jacket.)* Just stay here and when I get back we'll watch a movie. *(He lifts the oatmeal casket.)*

JENN. Say a prayer for it?

ERIC. I'll think of something.

JENN. His name is Rex.

ERIC. He has a name?

JENN. It's a male. When it was flopping in the back of the car, I hadda talk to him, and ...

ERIC. Rex. Fine. Now mourn quietly till I get back, and then we forget Rex forever. You got that, Jenn?

JENN. Yeah.

ERIC. No matter how much wine we drink we never tell this story at a dinner party ...

JENN. I swear. *(He leaves. She is sitting alone, staring.)* Goodbye Rex. *(Music: "Rex Tremendae"* chorus from the Mozart Requiem. Lights fade to black.)*

END

* See Special Note on Songs and Recordings on copyright page.

DIRTY TALK

CHARACTERS

ZEKE — young farmer.
WENDELL — older man in good shape; the bartender.
ELLIE — young woman, dressed as a rock star.

SETTING

A bar with a juke box and grade-school class photos all over the walls.

DIRTY TALK

At rise: Ellie is bent over the juke box.

ZEKE. Look at that ass. She ain't wearin' no panties. What the hell somethin' like that doin' in Somerville?

WENDELL. On her way to Chicago.

ZEKE. That's her limo out there waitin'?

WENDELL. She come out of it.

ZEKE. Chauffeur's gonna get frostbit.

WENDELL. Told her to bring him inside.

ZEKE. Them's New York plates. *(There is no response from Wendell.)* You got New York music in that box?

WENDELL. Supposed to be all kinds in there?

ZEKE. Well why ain't she playing her own kinda music?

WENDELL. Maybe country's her kind.

ZEKE. With an ass like that? No, she ain't country. *(He gestures to the bar window and looks out.)* How long's the chauffeur been sittin' out there?

WENDELL. Two hour so.

ZEKE. Musta' wasted ten gallons of gas.

WENDELL. He's warm.

ZEKE. What's she drinkin'?

WENDELL. Coke.

ZEKE. Then she must be doin' somethin' else along with it. Zollo and Charlie show up tonight?

WENDELL. Just left. Wishbone was here too.

ZEKE. Wishbone?

WENDELL. All left just 'fore you got here.

ZEKE. You mean Wishbone didn't try to have a little fun with her?

WENDELL.   She spurned 'im.

ZEKE.   Oh, no, sweetheart. You ain't shakin' that ass for your-self.

WENDELL.   She spurned Wishbone flat as a pancake.

ZEKE.   She ain't dancin' round here for nothing, Wendell. *(Ellie dances past Zeke.)* Hi ...

ELLIE.   *(Disinterestedly.)* Hi.

WENDELL.   Told ya. *(Zeke, a terrific dancer, moves in front of her and without touching her, does a perfect country two-step face to face with her. It amuses her, but she doesn't commit to dancing any closer. Suddenly she does a turn, leaving him dancing alone. He leans on the bar.)*

ZEKE.   She give me a hard-on worse than if she grabbed my balls. What time you closin'?

WENDELL.   Any minute. Can't take no chance and keep open past hours.

ZEKE.   Well, I'll be a mother's monkey! She's waitin' for you, Wendell.

WENDELL.   Git on.

ZEKE.   Can't you tell, man? You gonna' get laid, buddy.

WENDELL.   Not from no city trash. *(Zeke drinks his drink and throws a buck on the bar. He buttons up his coat, slips on his hat, and walks by her as if he's going to dare to reach out to touch her, but she eyes him with a cold challenge, continues dancing out of his reach, and he opens the door.)*

ZEKE.   'Night ... *(He exits.)*

ELLIE.   How come you only got grade-school graduation pictures up here?

WENDELL.   Don't wanna insult my customers.

ELLIE.   You got change for the juke box?

WENDELL.   You gimme dollars, I'll make you quarters 'til Hell freezes. You in the C.I.A.?

ELLIE.   Yes. *(She puts money in the juke box and sits at the table. Wendell brings her a Coke.)*

WENDELL.   This one's on me.

ELLIE.   'Bout time.

WENDELL.   Tell the truth. What you doin' in this town?

ELLIE. Breezin' through.

WENDELL. Breezin' ain't spending three hours in my bar.

ELLIE. Depends on your speedometer.

WENDELL. What's yours say?

ELLIE. Says I'm doin' ninety-five. How 'bout you?

WENDELL. My wagon's in the garage.

ELLIE. What's it take to get it out?

WENDELL. Nothin' much, if the time's right.

ELLIE. What's the time like now?

WENDELL. It's a funny in-between time.

ELLIE. Oh, yeah?

WENDELL. You a reporter doin' a story on this town?

ELLIE. What's there to report about this town?

WENDELL. Zero.

ELLIE. Would it make sense my reportin' on zero?

WENDELL. Well you know, typical America.

ELLIE. This is typical America? *(Laughs.)* No honey. You been livin' in your mind.

WENDELL. That driver of yours must be gettin' mighty cold out there.

ELLIE. He's got a heater.

WENDELL. Usin' up a lot of gas. You spendin' the night somewhere in this town?

ELLIE. Depends.

WENDELL. That's your last drink. I closed five minutes ago.

ELLIE. No fair.

WENDELL. This ain't New York.

ELLIE. Do you foxtrot?

WENDELL. How 'bout if I turn off these lights? *(He turns off main lights then grabs her.)*

ELLIE. Do you foxtrot?

WENDELL. I two-step.

ELLIE. That's good enough. *(They dance.)*

WENDELL. You married?

ELLIE. No. You?

WENDELL. Been.

ELLIE. Been married huh?

WENDELL. Don't I look like I been ... a couple times.

ELLIE. You look like more 'en a couple to me.

WENDELL. Right. You in one of them graduation pictures?

ELLIE. Not me.

WENDELL. You ain't from here, 'cept ...

ELLIE. 'Cept what.

WENDELL. I seen you ...

ELLIE. Oh yeah?

WENDELL. ... on TV or somethin'. *(His hands move down to her ass. She breaks away.)* You gonna spurn me, too?

ELLIE. You can touch, but don't squeeze. I'm not a squeeze box.

WENDELL. Touchin's fine with me. Let's go upstairs.

ELLIE. What's up there?

WENDELL. A bed.

ELLIE. There's chairs down here.

WENDELL. I ain't no contortionist.

ELLIE. I can sit on your lap.

WENDELL. You wanna show me how? *(Ellie puts a straight-back chair in the middle of the floor.)*

ELLIE. Sit. *(Wendell sits down, folds his feet; she lifts her wide skirt and mounts him as if he were a pony. They laugh face to face.)* Nice smell on your breath.

WENDELL. What's that?

ELLIE. Chesterfields.

WENDELL. Don't smoke Chesterfield. Smoke Winston.

ELLIE. Oh.

WENDELL. Useta smoke Chesterfield.

ELLIE. Uh huh. Oughta open your belt. *(Wendell laughs shyly, reaching under her skirt to undo his belt.)* Let them down. Let 'em down. *(He lets down his jeans.)*

WENDELL. Easy ... now.

ELLIE. Take time.

WENDELL. You're tight.

ELLIE. Be alright in a minute.

WENDELL. Ouch.

ELLIE. We're gettin' there.

WENDELL. Phew.

ELLIE. There ... there it is. Comfy now?

WENDELL. Not bad.

ELLIE. Let me get a look in your eyes.

WENDELL. What you see?

ELLIE. Real blue.

WENDELL. You like it?

ELLIE. Yeah, and crows feet crinklin' up around 'em.

WENDELL. Think I'm too old for ya?

ELLIE. Think I'm too young for you?

WENDELL. No, no. I'm set on getting old quick.

ELLIE. Why?

WENDELL. Wanna be like Willie Nelson.

ELLIE. He bores me.

WENDELL. Gonna let my hair grow, wear a kerchief 'round it.

ELLIE. What for?

WENDELL. Tired of the same thing all my life.

ELLIE. I like the way you look now.

WENDELL. Easy ... I come fast.

ELLIE. You're just bored.

WENDELL. Yeah, I guess.

ELLIE. You done it all.

WENDELL. Twice, three times around.

ELLIE. You done it this way much?

WENDELL. Too many times.

ELLIE. Mind doin' it one more time?

WENDELL. With you I can do it hundred more times.

ELLIE. How come?

WENDELL. Cuz you're a movie star.

ELLIE. I ain't.

WENDELL. Yes, you are ... a singer or something. How come you waited round here for me when you had your pick of studs the whole night ...

ELLIE. I figured you out.

WENDELL. Yeah?

ELLIE. For the best kisser.

WENDELL. Best kisser, huh?

ELLIE. Kiss me, Wendell. *(Wendell does.)*

WENDELL. Easy. I'm quick as lightnin'.

ELLIE. Don't be quick.

WENDELL. You're a talker. I ain't had one of you in a dog's age.

ELLIE. Talkin's half of it.

WENDELL. You got blue eyes.

ELLIE. Uh-huh.

WENDELL. Funny blue.

ELLIE. Like what?

WENDELL. Like chicory flowers ...

ELLIE. Nice color, but they shrivel up if you pick 'em.

WENDELL. You're a country girl.

ELLIE. Everybody knows chicory shrivels up.

WENDELL. Half the world don't know what a chicory flower *is*. I can't stand *this* much talk.

ELLIE. It ain't made you soft.

WENDELL. Nothing makes me soft, 'cept finishing.

ELLIE. You wanna finish?

WENDELL. Wouldn't hurt.

ELLIE. First let's improvise.

WENDELL.   What the hell is that now?

ELLIE. You play roles. Like, I'd be your little baby ...

WENDELL. Yeah?

ELLIE. And you ... you'd be my daddy?

WENDELL. Well, you start it off.

ELLIE.   Daddy, would you ... would you do something for me?

WENDELL. I sure would.

ELLIE. Pwotect me?

WENDELL. Protect you how?

ELLIE. 'Cawse I cowld. *(Wendell envelops her with his arms.)*

WENDELL.   How's this? You warmin' up? Huh, my sweetie pie?

ELLIE. Pwotect me from eweething bad.

WENDELL. I'm doin' that right now, honey bunch.

ELLIE. How?

WENDELL.   How you want me to?

ELLIE.   Put me inside your coat fowever.

WENDELL.   Okay. There's my coat around you.

ELLIE.   Now button it and carry me round with you fowever.

WENDELL.   I'd look pregnant.

ELLIE.   You'd have a pot belly.

WENDELL.   Okay. I'll carry you. How'm I doin?

ELLIE.   And would you keep kissing me without ever stop-ping?

WENDELL.   Well, I'd have to stop to breathe.

ELLIE.   Just to breathe, but otherwise, all one long kiss lastin' a whole six months, holdin' me in your arms and not lettin' me down except to tuck me in so you can go buy me a doll and bring it home to surprise me.

WENDELL.   A Barbie dolly.

ELLIE.   No. The old kind with eyes that blink.

WENDELL.   Okay then.

ELLIE.   And then wallpaper my room with paper full of tiny roses, and white curtains with pull-down shades that have little crocheted rings. And ... make me a trellis in the yard with yellow roses all over it.

WENDELL.   I made a rose trellis once round a whole gate with a fence ...

ELLIE.   And fuck me whenever I asked. And spank me if I was bad and bring me candy from Corwin's ...

WENDELL.   I ... I can't stand no more of this.

ELLIE.   Please Wendell, I just want you to say one more thing.

WENDELL.   Make it fast.

ELLIE.   Say ... I ... love you.

WENDELL.   But ...

ELLIE.   Like we was actors. You just have to act the words.

WENDELL.   I love you.

ELLIE.   You gotta look in my eyes.

WENDELL.   I love you.

ELLIE.   Not so *flat*. Say it with all your heart. I ...

WENDELL.   I love you.

ELLIE.   Oh, yes! That was it. Exactly. Do it ten times.

WENDELL.   Oh, come on!

ELLIE.   Ten times and we're all through.

WENDELL.   Love you, love you, love you ...

ELLIE.   Slow, like before.

WENDELL.   Love you. Love you.

ELLIE.   With the *"I"*: *"I"* ...

WENDELL.   I ...

ELLIE.   Love you, Ellie.

WENDELL.   Ellie?

ELLIE.   Yes. Ellie.

WENDELL.   I love you, Ellie.

ELLIE.   In my eyes now. Looka me.

WENDELL.   I love you, Ellie.

ELLIE.   Once more. Once more like that.

WENDELL.   What're you cryin' for?

ELLIE.   Please.

WENDELL.   I love you ... Ellie ... love you. Don't cry.

ELLIE.   You'll protect me?

WENDELL.   Sure, I'll protect you.

ELLIE.   And buy me a bag of root beer barrel candy from Corwin's.

WENDELL.   Corwin passed away.

ELLIE.   Oh...?

WENDELL.   Yeah. It's the laundermat now.

ELLIE.   No store there?

WENDELL.   No more store.

ELLIE.   Corwin's dead?

WENDELL.   You do come from here.

ELLIE.   Oh don't go soft on me. Kiss me.

WENDELL.   Now wait ... *(Ellie kisses him, getting him more and more excited.)* Miss ...

ELLIE.   Lemme ride you, Daddy.

WENDELL.   Jesus!

ELLIE.   Ride, Daddy. Oh yes, ride ...

WENDELL.   Slow down or I'll ...

ELLIE.   Wendell, I'm ready, ready if you are.

WENDELL. Christ! ... I'm ready.

ELLIE. Let's go together.

WENDELL. I'm gonna ... gonna ...

ELLIE. Together?

WENDELL. Uh huh.

ELLIE. Now?

WENDELL. Now.

ELLIE. Now? *(Overlapping with:)*

WENDELL. Oh God. Yes. Yes. Aggggg. Awww. Aw. Uhhh-mmm. *(Afterward.)* Jesus. Oh.

ELLIE. Stay still.

WENDELL. Ugg. Ouuuu.

ELLIE. Easy.

WENDELL. Ouuuuuuwheeee. Lemme outta this trap.

ELLIE. Not so fast.

WENDELL. Just wanna wash.

ELLIE. There's time.

WENDELL. Look, I wanna git decent here. *(He pulls up his trousers under her skirt, then tries buttoning them, but she doesn't get off.)* Lord a' mercy, will you let me stand up?

ELLIE. In a minute. Here, let me wipe your brow.

WENDELL. Who in the fuck are you?

ELLIE. One last look in the eyes.

WENDELL. I had enougha this.

ELLIE. One last kiss. Please. *(Wendell kisses her.)* Another ...

WENDELL. Shit.

ELLIE. One more. The last. The final. *(Wendell kisses her.)* And one last word. Say "goodbye."

WENDELL. Yeah. Goodbye ...

ELLIE. Ellie. Goodbye Ellie, darling.

WENDELL. Goodbye, Ellie. *(Ellie dismounts and starts putting on her coat.)*

ELLIE. I'm over there in that graduation picture ... 1967.

WENDELL. Yeah?

ELLIE. Second row. Fifth from the left.

WENDELL. Second row fifth from left? *(Checks photo.)* You whore, that's my son Billy.

ELLIE. They called me Billy round here once.

WENDELL. Now don't go insultin' my kinfolk.

ELLIE. I wouldn't insult Billy. I am Billy.

WENDELL. You get outta here you weirdo. Get outta my place. *(Ellie slips a quarter into the juke box.)*

ELLIE. I was put wise to you Wendell. One of your old wives. She said to me, "Billy, you want something from Wendell you gonna have to *steal* it 'cause he don't part with shit." So I stole. And I got.

WENDELL. You.... You ...

ELLIE. You think no man can do what I just did there? All it takes is a lil' operation.

WENDELL. You're pullin' somethin' on me.

ELLIE. Well ... you think what you want. I *got* what I want. Now I can go home for real.

WENDELL. Oh yeah? And where is that?

ELLIE. Oh it ain't a place, Daddy. It's a state of mind.

WENDELL. Dear Jesus. Lord, forgive me. You can't be Billy. Tell me you ain't Billy.

ELLIE. Second row, fifth from the left. That's me Wendell. Bye. *(The song she picked out on the juke box starts to play. Wendell stares as she leaves.)*

WENDELL. My dear Lord, Jesus Christ ...

END

CHARLIE'S FAREWELL

CHARACTERS

CHARLIE
BOOMER

CHARLIE'S FAREWELL

CHARLIE.   We are here to mourn the loss of ... of love. I mean to lose life is natural but to lose love ... is dangerous for the soul, murderous for the mind. I know this. Nothing throws us into darkness quicker than to lose our love ... or someone ... someone within whom ... what was I saying? Yes, it's like losing God. But we must forgive the dead, eh? They don't ask to die. They don't want to say goodbye and leave behind nothing but fragile little signs of the time they spent with us, a snapshot, a ring, a letter.... That's why I say woe to the living who kill love, who laugh at love, who tire of love, who fear it, are ashamed of it, who cheat on love, who steal it. Only they could get away with this, the dead just leave. They leave us to God.... But who is that, what is that? I'm not sure. Sorry ... she seems so helpless, she ... she seems not to be able.... Uh what was I talking about?
BOOMER.   God.
CHARLIE.   God. God, yes. God. No. I was talking about Judy, wasn't I? About if she were alive, how relieved, how freely we would all breathe! How safe we'd be, picnicking in the air, in the light in the sharp bright air, in the Spring Air, after all, it's Easter. If Judy were alive we'd smile again, we'd wear the dark clothes of Passover so death's angel would miss our door and leave us safe and huddled and unbroken in our hearts, unseparated but ... the angel didn't pass. The angel opened the door and walked away with Judy. Judy walked with the angel into a warm golden glow, leaving us alone in this hard light, incapable of going on, almost, incapable of saying ... goodbye. Our lips won't speak the word. We only can say, come back, come back Judy.... Come home. Judy.... What was I talking about?

MEN WITHOUT WIVES

CHARACTERS

POP
SON (BOOMER)

SETTING

The mudroom of an old Vermont farm house.

MEN WITHOUT WIVES

Pop is leaving after a two-week visit with his son, Boomer. They are saying good-bye in the mudroom, or pantry, off the kitchen of the son's old farmhouse near Bennington. This mudroom contains a small harvest table and a straight chair for putting on and taking off boots. Two dead Canadian geese, their heads hanging over the side, lie on the table near apples, pumpkins and some small glass jars of preserves with screw-on tops. Along with Pop's suitcase are his guns and his fishing pole, both obviously part of his gear that is going out the door with him. Pop is a "positive" thinker and an active person. His son, a professor, is more contemplative, gentler. He takes after his mother who, when she was alive, was generous and long suffering. She's gone a long time from their lives. Boomer holds the last jar of her jam in his hand. This jar is obviously older than the rest.

POP.   Don't leave those fish in the freezer more than a couple weeks.

SON.   I heard you.

POP.   Now there's six geese in your garage for the guy from the chicken farm, okay? He'll dress the deer right there. I left freezer paper for him. Don't tip him. And make him dress these birds in front of you, in the house, these are the best two. And if it appears the guy hasn't stolen some venison, let him have a steak or two. Did I tell you don't tip him? Then that's everything.

SON.   Take this jam with you ... *(Pop misses this gesture, leaving Boomer holding the jar.)*

POP.   You look a helluva lot better than when I pulled up to this place. *(He slings a bag over his shoulder.)* No more straining your eyes reading in this dark empty house. They couldn't pay me enough to be a damn schoolteacher.

SON.   What do you suggest I do?

POP.   Go see those maple leaves changin'. The trees are on fire. Stop messin' with people in books. They don't talk back for Chrissakes. Find some good woman who'll put a smile on your face.

SON.   Where?

POP.   Where? There's gotta be a bar somewhere in Vermont.

SON.   A bar.

POP.   Or go live back in the city, hang out at The Lion's Head again.

SON.   There's a whole new generation in the city.

POP.   Well ... I lost a wife once, too, you know.

SON.   She was my mother, remember? I lost her too.

POP.   She left me a son, didn't she? And look at the nice week we jus' had. You got a daughter in college now ...

SON.   What do I *do* in between finding a new job and scouting the bars up here for women who'll make me smile?

POP.   You always had a *mind* of your own. What's changed that all of a sudden?

SON.   You never lose that tongue of yours.

POP.   You're the one shunned business. You said you wanted to teach and to write.

SON.   You regret it, not me.

POP.   You're complainin', not me.

SON.   Because it's different up here with no Judy.

POP.   You want me to tell ya what really happened? You jus' got dealt out exactly what everybody gets. Sometimes it tastes bitter, but it's just life and death. Forget death. That takes care of itself. It's life that's the bitch. But you never learned to beat it on its own terms. You just parked your ass and sat down to write about how unlivable it is.

SON.   How did you beat life?

POP.   With this *brain* and this *rifle,* I'll survive whatever shit comes down. I can kill you, myself, anything, but I get the last word. I just left food enough to keep you alive for a month and it cost me nothin'. You don't even have to tip the guy who's gonna bloody his hands to clean it for you. I got brand new wheels out there. Teeth taken care of. A smile's a disease. People catch it. Next thing you know, you got all the action you can handle. I'm never lonesome in my bed. When I need a woman I don't *whine.* I get one. You know what I'm gonna do? Gonna leave this rifle ... *(Begins to open rifle case.)*

SON. No. Get it out.... *Take* it. Please.

POP. What're you 'fraid of?

SON. I'm not like you. I don't want to be like you.

POP. Well that's not news, is it, Boomer? *(Puts rifle back.)*

SON. Why'd you start smoking again?

POP. *(Laughs.)* If life's such crap, why're you so health conscious?

SON. I don't give a rat's ass for your health or mine.

POP. Now easy, Sonny ...

SON. It's just that you sat around here stinking up my house with smoke and drinking my Scotch and telling bad jokes for a week straight right after I bury my wife? Are you my father or Frank Sinatra?

POP. Come on ...

SON. Coming all the way up here to help me grieve, with goddamn guns and new shiny wheels parked out there to remind me of what I can't afford ...

POP. There's no competition in this.

SON. ... not that I would waste a nickel on the stuff that turns you on, if I had a nickel.

POP. You need money?

SON. Oh that's what you'd love. You tight ass. You let me pick up the check the two times we had dinner out. You sat around here honoring my dead while I taught class, and then you walked around *my* neighborhood killing every fucking thing that moves. I won't eat those poor animals. Are you crazy? I don't even want to see the doe hanging in my garage, dripping blood in the cement next to the oil stains.

POP. Sonny, wait ...

SON. *(Almost hysterical.)* I don't wanna hear "the herds need thinning." Let them die of starvation.

POP. Huh?

SON. I cooked vegetables here for ten days because that's

my perception of what's good for you. It cost me two hundred ... to stock the refrigerator and the bar ... and you know in that rotten heart of yours I'd slice my throat before taking a *nickel,* and you want me to admit that I'm poor.

POP.　You've gone mad, Boomer. Jesus. I'm sorry. *(Pop recognizes now that Boomer is in a lot of trouble. He reaches to touch his son.)*

SON.　Don't you *dare* try to touch me. Don't *dare* you pull that.

POP.　I came to take your mind offa Judy ...

SON.　My mother never would have married you today. Women are different. Thank God at last.

POP.　Oh, that's not right ... Dear Lord ...

SON.　And you have the nerve to come up here with guns. And comfort me with ... with dead birds? *(He throws the dead birds onto the floor.)* Leave them in the woods for the foxes, and I don't want your rotten money either. If you wanna give me something, give me an idea.

POP.　What're you talking about? What kind of idea?

SON.　*(Very excited, sarcastic.)* How do I know? I'm *asking* you. Leave me some kinda idea, before you go and have a heart attack in some trout stream.

POP.　*(Wiser, with caution.)* What's this idea involve?

SON.　It involves what everything is all about. It involves ... *(Confused.)* how to ... to figure out where I missed that turn ...

POP.　What turn?

SON.　I wake up feeling I'm supposed to be somewhere else.... *Home.* But I forgot where that is, like I took a wrong bus, and wound up here. My kid, she's some guy's lover. I'm not married anymore ...

POP.　Oh, Boomer.... You still have me ... *(Attempts to touch him.)*

SON.　*(Really screaming now.) Don't touch me.* None of that. We're old men. Old men.

POP.　Lord in heaven Boomer. Boomer ... *(Boomer is so disoriented now, shocked by his own behavior, he weakens, reaching behind himself for the hallway chair.)*

SON. Just go. I don't need you anymore.

POP. What can I do?

SON. Nothing. You're not the one ...

POP. Huh? Think of *anything.* Say it and by God I'll do it.
I'll *do* it.

SON. Just ... get me out of this mess.

POP. What mess are you in?

SON. Can't you see? This mess. *(Boomer cries.)*

POP. Explain the mess, son.

SON. You can't understand. It gets a certain kind of man ...
I'm afraid ... that I'm gonna kill myself in this old house.

POP. Okay. I believe it. Whatever ... *(Pop pulls out a handkerchief.)* Lemme wipe your forehead, here. *(Boomer resists.)*

SON. You can't I told you. It's too late.

POP. Oh, Boomer ... *(Pop kneels to the chair Boomer is sitting
in and, with difficulty, he embraces him.)*

SON. *No!* Goddammit.

POP. Please Boomer.... Let me.... Let me ... *(Boomer gives
in and allows it. He looks up, exhausted.)*

SON. Oh, God, how I hate being weak. How I hate taking
this from him. It's sick ...

POP. I know, Boomer. Don't be ashamed. Don't be ashamed.

SON. Oh, God ... Oh, God ... *(Repeats till almost inaudible.
Pop dries his son's forehead, pushing his hair back with each stroke.
Then he just holds Boomer tight around his waist, head down against
Boomer's chest, as if listening to his heart. Quiet descends. A beat.
Boomer blows his nose.)* Okay. Go and take this. *(Offers the jar of
jam again.)*

POP. I'm gonna stay a day or two more ...

SON. *No.* No Sir. You're on your way. C'mon. *(Loads Pop up
with his bags, then picks up the jar and sticks it in Pop's hand.)*
This is the very last jar of this stuff.

POP. *(Staring at the jar.)* No. I won't take Judy's last jar ...

SON. Look at the date. *(Pop puts on glasses, reads.)* It's not
Judy's.

POP. 1969? Oh Lord. Oh my dear Lord.

SON. Drive carefully.
POP. You sonofabitch. Sonofabitch. *(Lights fade.)*
SON. I'm sorry.

END

PARAKEET EULOGY

PARAKEET EULOGY

Robbie, a priest, is speaking straightforwardly to the audience. Near him is a bird cage covered with a cloth.

ROBBIE.   You want to be assigned a place in the heavens, you want a function, you want to have made a difference. You want to place a mark on time. You want protection, you want to believe you can die and not be embarrassed, that God has a brain, that you came from before and that you will exist beyond your death. You want to believe you're more than an insect that can be flippantly crushed by time. You want God to save you, you want God in the old fashioned way. You want him to be male, to be the father, you want to come home like the prodigal, you want his holy communion, his body, you want to eat his eternity. You want that glory, you wanna be bigger than you are, better than the animals. And when people leave you. And when the birds leave you when the summer ends, how you fear the cold, the advancing dark, because you say: "God doesn't have a brain." You feel the harmony, you feel the order, the system, you feel things are generally relative, you feel the earth is alive, the stars are alive, there's life out there but it's just not the father. It doesn't *think* like you or I. It's timeless, infinite but it has no heart.

So I made myself God ... to these little birds and they're trapped in my small life. I'm amazed by their intelligence you know? and their instincts, and they show gratitude. If I were to set them free here, they would perish in the cold, but I've learned of where they would survive very well, a place that still exists if man doesn't destroy it. Before I die, someday, I may take them there and set them free. Who knows? They might even show me the way.

END

EASTER NIGHT

CHARACTERS

PIA MONTEBELLO — An African-American professor at a small college in Vermont who has prepared Easter dinner at the Fox household. Judy Fox, her best friend, has died and earlier that afternoon there was a memorial service.

BOOMER FOX — Judy's husband, Boomer is middle aged. (His daughter Kristen is twenty one.) He teaches mathematics at the same small college.

KRISTEN FOX — A twenty-one-year-old senior at U. of Oregon. She's home for her mother's funeral.

CHARLIE PENNY — An Episcopal priest, chaplain to the college. He wears a cardigan sweater with his collar.

SETTING

The Fox dining room in their home in Vermont.

EASTER NIGHT

The play opens with the loud sound of a helicopter hovering over the house. The noise starts to recede as the actors speak. Pia is removing her pies from their boxes. Charlie is searching for something in the sideboard.

PIA.   Do you see a knife in there? I need to cut these pies.

CHARLIE.   Take it.

PIA.   What're you scratching for in there?

CHARLIE.   That blue ... sugar bowl ... of Judy's.

PIA.   I told you forget the sugar and don't ask him about it. He's worried his daughter is frozen in some snow bank and you're concerned about your next cup of joe.

CHARLIE.   I don't trust that kid. She's full of like ... anger. She sat stone-faced throughout my entire eulogy. A kid who doesn't cry at her mother's funeral? I'm sorry, that's spooky.

PIA.   She's pissed about him selling the house is what I think.

CHARLIE.   We're the ones who should be pissed.

PIA.   Did Boomer ever say anything to you about leaving Vermont?

CHARLIE.   Wouldn't I have told you?

PIA.   Well don't snap at me. It's disgusting. I mean.... It's unfair to us the more I think about it. He used us and now he's ...

CHARLIE.   Okay. Cool it. *(Boomer enters.)*

PIA.   Any word Boomer?

BOOMER.   They're taking the copter out of service because of the visibility. But I don't get it. The sun is out.

PIA.   It's the wind lifting the powder ... the snow. It's fine. It makes clouds ... like fog.

CHARLIE.   I'm telling you relax. She's out there doing ...

transcendental meditation or something in Buddha's little winter wonderland.

BOOMER.   C'mon Charlie. She just went through her mother's memorial service.

CHARLIE.   You know Boomer, she could be upset about something else.

BOOMER.   What do you mean? What else?

PIA.   Uh.... Pie anyone? Charlie? *(Warns him with her eyes.)*

CHARLIE.   I mean it rains a lot in Oregon, right? Well suddenly she's in fluffy white Vermont. The Snow Witch!

BOOMER.   What'd my daughter do to piss you off?

CHARLIE.   Your daughter has not got the power to piss me off Boomer, I never gave her that power. I gave it all to you.

BOOMER.   What's going on here? Pia?

CHARLIE.   Where's the damn sugar in this house?

BOOMER.   She has my wife's ashes. She took Judy's ...

PIA.   Oh no.

CHARLIE.   There's your answer. She's blowing Judy to the blizzard.

BOOMER.   It's ten below wind chill. Her coat's still here, okay Charlie? Her scarf, her gloves. Her hat is here. That's the thing.

CHARLIE.   Well she wasn't abducted, Boomer.

PIA.   May I say? I do think you may have thrown her.

BOOMER.   I? I threw her? How'd I throw her?

CHARLIE.   The way you threw us.

PIA.   He means ... about the house. That you're selling this house.

BOOMER.   I only told you. I wouldn't tell her I was selling the house she was born in on a day like this.

CHARLIE.   Oh. Well. We should be grateful.

BOOMER.   When you get sarcastic, I feel so ... totally let down. We're teachers in a college that's shutting down in what, two months?

PIA.   We've known the college was closing a long time.

BOOMER.   My wife died.

PIA.   And Judy was sick a long time and the thing is ... the three of us agreed.... We made plans to stay ... near you. Ohff.

CHARLIE. So where you going, Boomer?

BOOMER. Huh? New York? Boston? I ... I haven't even ...

CHARLIE. Who do you know there?

BOOMER. Nobody. Nobody.

PIA. You'd throw yourself at strangers when there are people here who ... who.... Oh never mind.

BOOMER. People here who what? Say it.

PIA. Care ...

CHARLIE. You set us up, Boom Baby.

BOOMER. How'd I set you — set you up for what?

PIA. Charlie's taking a parish here. He could have gone to another campus. It's that.... We ... we were like family. *You* said *that*. I signed a contract to teach at the high school. Why do you think I did that? You said you would write full time, finish your novel.

BOOMER. Pia, Darling. Please, my kid's out there in ten below, the sun is low and I'm in no mood for this at the moment.

CHARLIE. It's not just low.

BOOMER. What.

CHARLIE. The sun. It's down.

BOOMER. Now I'm worried. Now I'm really worried. You don't think she's ... you don't think she's capable of ... you know.

PIA. We're all capable of that. No, I don't think she's the kind. *(Kristen is back. Offstage she is stamping snow off her feet.)*

BOOMER. What's that? Is it...?

PIA. I think it's her. Wait.

CHARLIE. Don't listen to me.

BOOMER. God. Please let it be.

KRISTEN. *(From off.)* Papa?

PIA. Don't make a fuss. *(Kristen enters dressed in an elaborate formal wedding gown, also wearing jeans and boots. Around her neck is a ribbon with two white satin wedding shoes hanging from each end. She carries a bouquet of bare twigs and a Walkman in hand.)* Ho.... Gee.... Kristen!

BOOMER. Do you realize there was a police helicopter scouring these woods looking for you?

KRISTEN.   For me? I was wearing these. *(Walkman and head set.)*
BOOMER.   What the hell are you supposed to be and where the hell have you been?
PIA.   You look enchanting but you must be frozen.
CHARLIE.   What ... for? What's the idea?
KRISTEN.   I'm in my winter camouflage.
CHARLIE.   Is this her wedding gown ... or ... who's is it?

BOOMER. *(Overlap.)*	KRISTEN. *(Overlap.)*
My wife's.	It was my ... mother's.

CHARLIE.   I told you. The Snow Witch.
BOOMER.   Take that dress off, please. Take it off.
KRISTEN.   Mom said it's mine.
BOOMER.   To get married in.
KRISTEN.   To do anything I want in. It's mine. It's miiiine. *(She spins.)*
PIA.   But tell us, we're curious. Why on a day like, you know, your mother's...?
KRISTEN.   To keep me warm in a way that ... you may not appreciate.
CHARLIE.   Pia, I'm tired. You ready?
BOOMER.   No. Have coffee. No, I insist. Charlie needs the sugar. He can't find it.
KRISTEN.   Don't look at me. I don't live here.
PIA.   I think you'd better take off your Mom's dress before it ...
KRISTEN.   It's already ruined.
BOOMER.   Kris ...
KRISTEN.   Her whole marriage is ruined. It's dead. Right?
BOOMER.   What a rotten thing to say.
KRISTEN.   Till death do us part, Man. You're free. Freedom is everywhere today.
BOOMER.   Take it off, Kristen. Please.
KRISTEN.   Oh ma' God do I look like her or something? By the way, who packed Judy's clothes so neatly in all those neat cartons? I'll bet it was neat and efficient Pia.
PIA.   That's right.
KRISTEN.   Thank you so much. And was it Pia who washed

down her closets with Lysol, everything scrubbed clean and ready for the local revolution? Her perfume's gone from the dresser.

PIA. *(Overlap.)* She gave it to me.

KRISTEN. Why didn't you take the wedding dress? Did I say something?

PIA. Why'd you put it on today?

KRISTEN. Oh, simple. I thought, here's mother's beautiful wedding gown with no mother in it, and here's her ... her ashes. I would have dressed the corpse in something like this, so I could see her one last time but when I got here she was all fried. The decisions all had been made by whomever thought they had the right. So I figured ... let me just ... pour Judy back into her shoes and ...

BOOMER. You didn't.

KRISTEN. ... and I brought them high up on the ridge. The helicopters should have seen me there, the sky was blue, the sun was out. I turned her shoes upside down and she blew away. Boom! a momentary grey cloud and then all white again. No sick Judy anymore no bones just ... just me now. The dress fits but these don't. Who is Cinderella? Is it you, Charlie?

BOOMER. Very funny. Let's have dessert. Where's your mom's sugar bowl?

KRISTEN. How should I know? I hate sugar.

CHARLIE. It wasn't in the kitchen, Pia?

PIA. Unless I'm going blind.

CHARLIE. I can't take a night like this without a cup of java. So I think I'll take off.

BOOMER. Can't you give up coffee for one day?

CHARLIE. I gave up alcohol. Gave up cigarettes. If I give up coffee tonight I might murder somebody.

KRISTEN. Aren't you worried that "Your Lord" will tire of your whining?

CHARLIE. Like Clark Kent my whining ceases when souls jump out of flaming skyscrapers. I throw off my glasses and make the rescue. But who will catch me when I fall? Ha haaa.... Nobody around here.

KRISTEN. Put your trust in Jesus.

CHARLIE. If I was your father you know what I'd do to you?

KRISTEN. And if I was my father I'd kick your ass out of here.

BOOMER. Stay right where you are Charlie.

KRISTEN. I mean there's not even existential emptiness to his humor, it's just bad.

CHARLIE. What is God trying to teach me here?

KRISTEN. To shut up.

BOOMER. You're not gonna talk like this to your mother's friends.

CHARLIE. She's not? What's gonna stop her Boomer? You? The lamb was great. *Merci beau coup! Au revoir ...*

PIA. Hold it Charlie.

KRISTEN. Don't leave on my account. I'm going.

PIA. But we haven't heard your news.

CHARLIE. Pia ...

PIA. You graduate in two months?

KRISTEN. I graduate. Yes.

PIA. Then what?

KRISTEN. How can I know what's going to happen to my life any better than you know what's gonna happen to yours?

BOOMER. She's right isn't she?

KRISTEN. Look at you! The essence of Koyaanisqatsi.

BOOMER. See it through.

CHARLIE. Do you mind if I pretend she's not here?

BOOMER. Cool it, Charlie.

KRISTEN. I'm so ashamed of you.

PIA. What did we do, Sweetie?

KRISTEN. You're all part of the Koyaanisqatsi.

CHARLIE. That's a little town in Maine?

PIA. World out of balance.

CHARLIE. How minimal-zen-tres-chic-avant ... *out!*

PIA. And we're the world?

CHARLIE. She's the world.

KRISTEN. *(Chanting.)* Koyaanisqatsi.

CHARLIE. Oh, please this is so embarrassing ... *(Beat.)* She's directing it to me for some anti-clerical reason. *(Beat.)*

PIA. Sit down Charlie. Kris, come, have some coffee. C'mon.

BOOMER.   I'm gonna find that sugar bowl.

PIA.   Boomer, forget it.

CHARLIE.   Philip Glass gimme a break. Is the world *still* out of balance? Haven't we fixed something?

PIA.   What do you see here? An African-American cutting Easter cake in WASP snow heaven, a gay Episcopal minister ...

CHARLIE.   Hey ...

PIA.   ... who's equally out of place. I mean ... how did we?

BOOMER.   How'd we what?

PIA.   Come so far into nowhere?

KRISTEN.   Why don't you all go back?

BOOMER.   Kris ...

PIA.   Back in time or back to Africa?

KRISTEN.   I'm not a racist.

CHARLIE.   I think we need a couple of coats here.

PIA.   We'd be more useful throwing our bodies at the bull dozers in Brazil at this point.

KRISTEN.   I don't think either choice will make much difference although the air might be cleaner around here if you all got lost in some rain forest.

BOOMER.   Go to your room. Get outta here.

PIA.   No Boomer. Please.

CHARLIE.   You afraid of Koyaanisqatsi? Wait till you see what's coming. There's a thunderous big noise about to sound out there. I'm getting our coats. *(He exits offstage to where the coats are.)*

PIA.   So Kris, does this mean we won't see you for a while?

KRISTEN.   I'll be inventing yet another life, like you all have done. I like Oregon. It's my home, I just discovered.

PIA.   Keep up your photography. You're good.

KRISTEN.   Don't play art-mother with me, bitch.

PIA.   Don't move Boomer. I'll see this out.

BOOMER.   We.... We didn't discuss the new Streep movie.

PIA.   That's right. We were going to.

CHARLIE.   *(Re-entering with coats.)* I liked her. I love her.

PIA.   She reminds me of a stereo sound demonstration tape. I can come from the left, or would you like the right? I am Polish princess. I am Ironweed Bum. I get syphilis in Africa,

Italian girl ...

KRISTEN. Jealous bitch.

BOOMER. Shutup.

PIA. Why wouldn't I be jealous of her? Of course I'm jealous of her.

KRISTEN. He burned his novel.

PIA. That isn't all he burned, Honey. He burned my ass.

CHARLIE. I'm outta here.

BOOMER. Don't you dare walk out on me like that.

KRISTEN. Ou ... you're all in love.

BOOMER. Huh?

PIA. Hey you, Judy was my best friend. I didn't go robot on her when she died.

BOOMER. Jesus, Pia.

KRISTEN. And I felt nothing? I didn't know my nerve endings registered in your body.

PIA. You think you're a glib little bundle of action don't you? Well I got your number, kid. You're a trouble making little Skinhead is what you are. You take me on girl, you gonna lose.

KRISTEN. I consider myself an adult so I'm gonna say something that may sound rude coming from what you consider a "kid," but mind your own fucking business. I don't buy your primal crying shit, your resurrection of the body bogus lies. I am a goddamn robot because I'm okay that my mother died, that I can celebrate it in my own untraditional cosmic way?

CHARLIE. Just don't sound too happy about it.

KRISTEN. Do I look too happy?

CHARLIE. Oh come out from your Ayn Rand bubble.

KRISTEN. This is a dinner party at my house, this is still, in some moral way, my house. *(To Boomer.)* Isn't it?

BOOMER. Of course it's your ...

KRISTEN. Is she fucking you?

PIA. Who the hell do you think you are?

KRISTEN. Or is he? *(To Charlie.)* I could kick both your asses out of here.

BOOMER. No, you couldn't.

KRISTEN. She doesn't have the right to talk to me that way

in a restaurant, much less my mother's house. So, okay, I'm not kicking your ass out of here. I'm simply telling you, you are full of shit about why people don't cry. I don't view life in your hippie way, how could I? I'm young.

PIA.   What's antiquated about crying at a funeral?

KRISTEN.   I hope you get herpes from some hot tub.

PIA.   My hippie days are over. You're the one moving to hot tub heaven. Your turn in the tub, Baby. You sweat.

CHARLIE.   *(Taking Pia's coat from her.)* Your arm. Stick it … in here.

PIA.   We all have our own little personal Koyaanisqatsi? You know what yours is? Your mother is dead.

KRISTEN.   Like I don't know.

BOOMER.   Pia …

PIA.   That's right. You turned it into something else. Spite. Jealously. Drama.

CHARLIE.   We gotta get up early.

PIA.   You're number one now. You blow away her ashes without letting anyone know. That's not about the dead, Sweetie. That's about us. Stealing our grief. That's about somebody's ego. And cosmic my ass, by the way.

KRISTEN.   You're all twice as dead as she is. You sit around my dinner table like you were in some cabinet shaping the world with cheap liberation theology … ecology, anti-nuke, hippie bullshit. You whine and go back to your classrooms to teach semi-retarded middle-class kids how to whine and surrender their lives to the military industrial complex. But finish a novel? Show Meryl Streep how it's really done? No. The closest you come to action is the black smudges of newsprint on your fingers every morning. Meantime, another world of people make fortunes, take power, kill, let live, rape, or set free the world and you wrap yourselves in plaid scarves up in snowy Vermont, sit on your asses and surf the Internet.

PIA.   What am I listening to this for?

BOOMER.   Let her finish.

KRISTEN.   Those guys on the moon, looking back at the Earth, don't you think their minds didn't get *fucked?* You think they were thinking of profit or Meryl Streep and this dish and

Judy's death? Looking back at the ball of Earth you think they could see our precious Judy or any of us? It's Gaia ...
CHARLIE. Oh no.
KRISTEN. Hundred million years breathing in, hundred million breathing out, not forty-seven years old like my mom. What *doesn't* die in a hundred million...? All of us, the ice cap, the polar cap ... they found alligator fossils ...
CHARLIE. Excuse us ... *(Boomer gestures for them not to leave.)*
KRISTEN. They drill a ... a ... cylinder two hundred feet in the snow and they find air from millions of years ago, preserved air, and it was different, nitrogen oxide, which is why I don't miss or mourn my mother ... or collapse into tears any more than I'd miss that school teacher that blew up in the ... thing. The Cape. Space. Canaveral ... because she couldn't have lived forever either and I ...
BOOMER. You brought home your laundry.
KRISTEN. What the hell is that?
BOOMER. It's sitting in the cellar for two weeks now. Is Gaia gonna do it, or are you expecting a glacier to pull your socks and pantyhose down to the equator?
KRISTEN. I was waiting for Judy to do it.
CHARLIE. I'm gonna warm up the car ...
BOOMER. No. Don't leave me alone with her.
PIA. I'll stay. Go warm up the car. *(Charlie exits.)*
KRISTEN. I drove a fucking pickup ... a goddamn ... fucking shitbox second-hand pickup truck from fucking Oregon ...
BOOMER. You know what this house is like when it's empty? Month after month after month? It's not the place you remember. You went back to school, she was ashes in a ... a *box* on the mantel and I'm floating in the whistling air, through ten rooms.
KRISTEN. Crying your poor eyes out.
BOOMER. Waking up sweating every night.
KRISTEN. So which one came over to comfort you?
BOOMER. I'm not having anything with any of them.
KRISTEN. They don't think so. I had to learn you're selling the house from some real-estate creep who came to the

door yesterday with people ...

BOOMER. Oh no. Oh God. So that's it. Did you let them in?

KRISTEN. They tip-toed around your empty wine bottles. I don't think they dug the house. Prices have crashed you know.

BOOMER. Kris I ...

KRISTEN. Don't you touch me.

BOOMER. Don't tell me that. I'll touch you all I like. I'll kiss you. I'll put you over my knee. You're my daughter.

KRISTEN. Just like your father. You hate to hear that don't you? What's it, ten years till you get your cancer ticket? Maybe fifteen?

BOOMER. You cruel ugly kid. If I don't tell myself I'm young enough to start over I'm dead here. I'm exactly where you are except not twenty-one anymore. Why don't you ... why don't you come to New York with me.

KRISTEN. Oh, don't fuck it up.

PIA. Goodnight all. (*He calls after Pia.*)

BOOMER. Pia ... *I started a new novel! (But she's gone, so to Kristen.)* I did. I ...

KRISTEN. What's it to me? You insisted you're a writer, not us. We just surrendered to it. The imperial voice narrated and Judy got up and made him tea and sandwiches as a reward for having himself. For a decade you sent me to my room to drown in television while my mother sat down here editing cartons of words, words you just burned anyway, like you burned her.

BOOMER. She asked to be cremated.

KRISTEN. I didn't want that ...

BOOMER. She requested it ...

KRISTEN. ... I wanted her under the ground *safe*, I wanted to imagine her face in the dark, frozen, perfect, as white as ice, as white as clouds, not ashes in a box. I went out to see how it feels to be that cold. I wanted to be as close to death as possible, where she is, in air so cold that nothing bad could live in it ... like heaven. Near her. Don't touch me. Let me have this anger, please. It's all I have right now. Go. Tell them I'm sorry. Tell them I'm sorry. Go Dad. (*Boomer runs out.*

Kristen is alone on stage. She clicks on her head set without put-ting it on. Music comes in. loud over the house speakers [Koyannisqatsi]. She goes to the sideboard, opens the door, and re-moves the blue sugar bowl. With the flavor of a sacrament, Kristen sits at the middle of the table. She bows down, arms encircling, em-bracing loosely the blue sugar bowl. The Koyannisqatsi theme builds over the house speakers as she straightens up and removes the cover from the blue sugar bowl. A faint light rises out of the bowl. Pia, Boomer and Charlie return and are stunned to see what they see. Upon seeing them, Kristen returns the cover to the sugar bowl. and with that there is a simultaneous blackout and a simultaneous change in music. Upbeat.)

END

FIAT

CHARACTERS

KENNETH — haircutter in Emil's Coiffure Shop.

MADONNA — a really coo-coo woman with a Brazilian accent, fantastically dressed in a truly fabulous, bird-influenced outfit of spangles, luminous fabrics, and feathers. She appears to be the wealthiest, best-dressed, bad-taste prostitute, wearing such things as red pearlescent spike-heel shoes, white anklets over roll-up stockings, orange feather boa, neon tights, with a stretch-tube halter, sparkler make-up and so forth.

SETTING

A hairdressing establishment in a Gold Coast, urban neighborhood.

FIAT

Kenneth is on the phone, talking to his partner. We may hear the tinny buzz of Emil's voice through the phone speaker.

KENNETH.   I'll stick the goddamn scissors in my neck, okay? And you can shove my share of this sleazy hair factory right between those twisted buns of yours and clean up her hair and my blood with the same dirty rag. *(Pause.)* Emil, what do I care she knows Angie Dickinson? You're lucky I even remember who she is Angie Dickinson, have you been dead the past twenty years? I should give a rotten rat's ass about a punk elephant bitch who knows Angie Dickinson in the last ten minutes of my life? I got blue lumps in my neck, blue lumps in my groin, my tongue is white, something red is growing on my belly and I am not the American Flag. I got you moaning in my ear, some bitch is suing me over nothing less than a haircut and you're telling me the Gods don't beckon from Valhalla? *(Pause.)* Of course the business is ruined. This is a punk barber shop, is it not? So why'd the woman walk in here? Oh don't give me I'm scared of women and that's why I'm gay. Do you wonder why I quit your crazy shrink? Good-bye, Shitball. Good-bye to Angie, to that litigious bitch who claims to know her....Why? I told you why. Disgust, Emil, disgust, you maniac putana. Jesus, Mary, and Joseph, help me. *(The Madonna enters.)* Emil, I got another one. New. No. Worse. *(Cups phone.)* We're closed, Ma'am. *(He gives her his back, assuming she's on her way out. The Madonna uses the audience as a mirror to roll her stockings up over her pearlescent tights, and to test various lengths.)* Emil, I don't care if you don't believe I'm capable of doing what I said ... *(With the phone couched in his neck he opens pill containers, checking.)* I got enough Seconals to destroy the whole elephant species on the planet, okay? I got six scissors ... over forty Valiums plus, by sheer coincidence I have a razor in my hand. I'm *carne morte*, Emil. I do too know where the artery is. *(Pause.)* Emil, blood is no big deal, you stop at Gristedes you get Fantastic.... Do it on the sidewalk? Why? I will *not* do it on the sidewalk in front of everybody out there. *(Pause.)* So. You pick up a bag of sponges in D'Agostinos. They're on sale ... *(The Madonna is now using the audience to practice what could be a nightclub act.)*

MADONNA.   A tico tico teek, a tico tico tock, a tico tico tico tico tico tock. And when it says coo coo it means it's time to woo a tico tico tico tico tico tock. A tico tico teek ...

KENNETH.   Ahem. Thee shop is closed. I cannot take care of you, Miss.

MADONNA.   I pay you duuubel.

KENNETH.   I'm killing myself. I'm performing a disgusting act that will make you seek. *Mal.*

MADONNA.   I break you perdon?

KENNETH.   *(Into phone.)* It's that ... Carmen Miranda clone dressed like a Fiorucci klepto.

MADONNA.   A tico tico tic ... *(She goes on.)*

KENNETH.   What does she want, Emil? Do we sell kiwis? Do we groom poodles? She wants a *haircut! (Grabbing her by the arm and leading her to the door.)* I tico take your arm, I taco lead you out, I tico tico tico tacky lock dee door. And if you say no no. I keek you weet dees toe. And if you sue me I won't be around to know. *(Throws her out and locks the door. Back on the phone.)* Emil, tell her you'll give her one of those chic baldies. Pay for the earrings. *(Pause.)* What? No, I did not take my Valium. *(Idea!)* Yet! *(Grabs his Valium bottle, takes one, considers, makes it the whole container, then downs the Seconals.)* Ah, yes, I'll feel much better in ten minutes. Well, I'll say goodbye now darling. Worry about your glands without me, worry about every fart alone, cheri, because your Kenneth jumped out of the dirigible, honey. He's in the air without a ... *(Ken shrieks. The Madonna is back inside.)* Oh ma-god she gave me such goose bumps. The Bongo Princess just walked through the door. *(Pause.) Through* theeee doooor Emil. *(Pause.)* It was *locked* Emil, *that's* what's so unusual. A despairing man *can so* get goosebumps. Madam … *(He cups the phone.)* How did you do that?

MADONNA.   A tico tico tic, a little sheer magique, a little supernatu, naturalitee. 'Cause when you go coo coo, comes then the time for who? For me to catch you 'cause you call the name of Gee. *(Chorus.)* Of Geesu-Geesu-Geesu Joseph and Maria! I come to catch you 'cause you call for me to see ya. Or else you might go to hell and you will not feel so well. It's such the pits you might as well have stayed right here …

KENNETH.   *Stop! I'm Jewish.*

MADONNA.   I Jewish, too. Blassit Veeergin.

KENNETH.   You're the blessed Virgin Mary?

MADONNA.   You called me. Heysus, Choseph, and Maria. Me.

KENNETH.   Where are the other two?

MADONNA.   Choseph, that's his beezneez. I nayvair interfere. Heysus? He may show up berry berry soon. *(Kenneth picks up the phone.)*

KENNETH.   Emil, did you hang up? He did. She's not here. It's the pills. Where's the razor?

MADONNA.   Me girlfriend tole me jou gotta go see thees saxy man who cots air.

KENNETH.   Me?

MADONNA.   Jou are biyouteefool. Yeah.

KENNETH.   Oh Emil, I'm in a Hector Babenco movie.

MADONNA.   Saxy beyond beleeef. Come, we make the Pieta.

KENNETH.   The Pieta statue? *(Madonna tears off her top and bares her breasts.)*

MADONNA.   We make it real.

KENNETH.   Oh these Seconals are tacky. Put your tits back, I hate tits.

MADONNA.   Oh…. De woman's body lets dee world go on. You no want dee world to and?

KENNETH.   Let it end, let it end. Oh, let it go on.

MADONNA.   It's hokay my body eees like thees?

KENNETH.   Why men go crazy over tits I'll never know.

MADONNA.   You know. You inside here for nine month. You suck you mommy teet. You remember?

KENNETH.   I forgot honey, and it wasn't no accident.

MADONNA.   I make you remember when you *like* it. *(She sits to a distant sound of supernatural voices, angels, transfiguration music, thunder.)*

KENNETH.   Oh my God, she can do it.

MADONNA.   Come Kenneth, come on now. *(Here the actors may gradually change, coming from behind their comic masks. She speaks in a perfect North American accent. His voice becomes unaffected, dropping a few octaves.)*

KENNETH.   Am I dying?

MADONNA.   Yes. You may pass through me.

KENNETH.   Don't they have a male representative?

MADONNA.   You don't have to be funny anymore.

KENNETH.   Oh, Emil, I hate these bitches.

MADONNA.   Liar. *(She unfurls a silvery-blue metallic smock, which she ties at her neck, the kind they use for customers, only here, it takes on aspects of the marble folds in Michaelangelo's Pieta.)* You touch women for nine, ten hours a day, our hair, our faces, caressing, pampering, making beautiful. Why does a man touch women so much if he doesn't love us? I see by your eyes you remember now, don't you? You remember.

KENNETH.   Yeah ... I remember.

MADONNA.   Remove your clothes and present your Buddha nature.

KENNETH.   Oh, these pills ...

MADONNA.   Risk it Ken. You'll come out new and fresh on the other side.

KENNETH.   Why don't all those straight people risk jumping in my lap?

MADONNA.   Oh they will, they'll have to. Everyone will have to pass through everything. Let go, before it's too late, quick, and you'll be far away from here, far away and free.

KENNETH.   Free to do what?

MADONNA.   To enter timelessness, to live again.

KENNETH.   Is this my bar-mitzvah or my confirmation?

MADONNA.   This is your death.

KENNETH.   Okay ... I'm going to go with this, okay? *(He

removes his clothes. We hear lions roar, jungle sounds, birds and transformational music. Kenneth climbs onto her chair. Take me back … (They kiss as lovers would kiss.) Take me home. (She lifts her blue tent and he curls up in her lap. Gradually, he dies in her arms, forming a tableau of Michaelangelo's Pieta. As lights on them fade, their images darken to a silhouette.)

END

PART II

LIGHTNING

CHARACTERS

WOMAN
CHILD

SETTING

Bare stage. The Woman's soiled frontier dress and her rustic chair are realistic.

LIGHTNING

The woman sits with a large, American family Bible in her lap. She's soaked to the skin in an open field, having just sat through a lightning storm filled with tornadoes, rain and hail. The storm has passed through her farm leaving her and her nearby house untouched though it is now ravishing a field close by as it departs.

From the storm's inception she had been sitting under the sky, challenging God to find her and destroy her. She sits on an old farm chair in a drenched house dress and apron, exhausted from chores but now, somehow refreshed. For a while the audience may believe they are watching a wordless play full of sounds of an approaching storm which arrives and shows us it's powerful heart and then departs, leaving nothing but calm in it's wake. The woman stares out over the audience during this until soft winds arrive, a bird chirps and it seems the piece is ending. Just then, a child sings out.

CHILD. Mama ... *(The Child appears, a girl of twelve, throwing herself upon the Woman who still sits stunned and wet in the old chair.)* Come inside, Mama. Grandma's cryin'. She can't get outta bed.
WOMAN. In a minute. Get away.
CHILD. He didn't take ya. Thanks for not takin' her. C'mon. Billy said he's sorry. No need to sit out here.
WOMAN. He did nothin'.
CHILD. I gave him a whack.
WOMAN. No.... You shouldn't.
CHILD. I gave Lissy her bottle. I ... heated the milk. And I changed Harry's diaper.
WOMAN. Not yours to trouble with.

CHILD. And I washed off the wall near his crib.

WOMAN. Don't. *(She puts arms around the child protectively.)*

CHILD. What makes him write on the wall with his poo poo?

WOMAN. Shhhh. *(She presses the child to her, rocking her.)*

CHILD. And I told Billy it weren't your fault Pa left. Pa's a bad man.

WOMAN. Hush. Quiet.

CHILD. Come inside, Ma. Ma?

WOMAN. Shhhh.

CHILD. It's all wet and it's chilly.

WOMAN. Alright. *(She stands and puts an arm around the child, who leads her, as if she were the parent.)*

CHILD. I prayed the lightnin' won't touch ya.

WOMAN. Did you?

CHILD. Lord must listen to me.

WOMAN. Do you think so?

CHILD. Every time you do this, I pray he'll pass you over.

WOMAN. I'm still here.

CHILD. So praise the Lord. Right, Mama? Well, right? Praise the Lord?

WOMAN. *(Bitterly.)* Come inside. Come with me ... *(They exit together. Blackout.)*

END

120

BIRD OF ILL OMEN

CHARACTERS

DOREEN — is thirty-five.

SPOOK — is fifty or over. He reads lips, since he is deaf.

SETTING

A room in a trashy whorehouse near Times Square, in New York City.

BIRD OF ILL OMEN

At rise, the phone rings. Doreen reaches from her bed and picks up the alarm clock, looks at it, puts it clumsily back on the bed table, then lifts the telephone receiver, bringing it under the covers to her head.

DOREEN.   My God! What are you doin'? It's only eleven o'clock in the morning. *(Pause.)*
   Well, get rid of him. What is this, some joke? Tell him I'm resting. *(Pause.)*
   No. How do you know it's him? *(Her head comes up.)*
   My God, you didn't accept his money! *(Pause.)*
   I don't give a hoot what Richie said, you get on the elevator and stop this creep from coming up here. *(She sits up.)*
   Where is Richie now, on what floor? Oh yeah? *(She throws the phone, grabs her robe, and runs to the door.)*
   Goddamn.... Son-of-a ... *(She pulls the door open and there stands Spook, a tall man dressed as if it is cold outside. His hand is raised as if to knock. He wears a long black overcoat and hat, seedy, formal, yet he is beautiful somehow, a once-handsome fellow. We can see that this man carries an old wound. His eyes, especially, are those of one who has tolerated a deep grief of many years. He has a love of Doreen that is instantly apparent, and an understanding of her anger. The audience may wonder: Is he her father, an old lover, her husband, school teacher, older brother? But his relationship to her will be as lost to us as his voice and hearing are to him. When she opens the door and sees him, she is at first shocked into speechlessness. With recognition, she begins to laugh, mockingly, hysterically, closing the door so as not to disturb the other girls.)*
   Where did you get that coat? *(Spook laughs with her.)*
   And that hat? *(He takes off the hat and she stops laughing when she sees his hair.)*

My God! You've gone all gray! You're an old man. *(He starts to take off his overcoat.)*

Hold it! *(Serious.)*

I'm on resting time, you hear? You got no right to bust in on me here, and you're gonna leave in five minutes. You hear? *(He merely pulls off his scarf. She grabs a cigarette. He hovers clumsily nearby. Doreen starts waking up.)*

You're a hoot and a half comin' here. I hope you're satisfied with what you see. Glamorous, isn't it? I don't want any sermons. *(He reassures her with a smile.)*

And I don't want to hear any bad news about anybody. And I don't want you touching me. I'm serious about that. In five minutes, out. *(He agrees. Doreen sits at her dressing table, looking into the audience or mirror.)*

You are a hoot and a half. Wasting your money. What's it supposed to do? You think you'll get me to walk out of here with you? *(He indicates no.)*

Oh yeah? *(She stays sitting, putting on lipstick. He hovers, still in place, like a little boy put in the corner by his teacher. His presence should be mysterious. His immobility should transcend her nervousness, his silence should transcend her chatter.)*

If something serious happened to anybody, I ... I don't want to know about it. Please ... I couldn't stand it right now. *(He doesn't react.)*

Okay? Or if somebody got married, or ... or maybe died in the Army or anything like that, I don't want any part of it. What good would it do me to know? *(She gives in to her worries, facing him, meekly asking.)*

Is somebody in trouble? *(He shakes his head no.)*

Nobody died? *(No.)*

Thank God. Oh thank God. *(She picks up her brush to brush her hair, hesitates, and throws it down.)*

Do you realize what you've just put me through, you creepy crut-faced idiot? Coming in here like the spook that you are? What do you want? *(No reaction.)*

I hope you didn't think you could fuck me. *(Shakes his head no.)*

To borrow money? *(No.)*

Just to get a look at me? Well here she is sweetie. *(She spins.)*

A little thigh? *(Opens her robe.)*

A little ass? A shoulder? *(He looks on with sadness.)*

A coupl'a Motown movements? Remember this? You like that, huh? *(She moves up close to him, as if he were a wild beast standing there. She drinks in his face.)*

Christ, did you get old. What are you doing here? What did you come here for, Spook? *(He looks down, shyly.)*

Somethin's on your mind. Somethin' serious? About someone I love? Is it one of my kids? *(No.)*

You're sure now? *(He crosses his heart, tears come; he wipes his eyes bravely. She sits, thinks.)*

Is it you? It is you. What's the matter? Well, don't stand there looking like you swallowed a football. Are you sick? *(Her voice is mean and commanding, but she's frightened, really. He gestures, yes.)*

Is it contagious? *(He didn't get the word.)*

Catching. Is it catching? *(He understands. Assures her: no, not catching.)*

Then is it … you know, that you can die from it? *(He waits, as if it's difficult for him to admit, then he indicates yes.)*

Can it happen … soon? *(He shrugs. Then he shakes his head: yes.)*

Well, what the hell do you want from *me?* *(He stares, scared of the terror she masks with pretensions of hardness.)*

What can I do for you? Aren't I miserable myself? Alone here? Who worries about me here? Huh? Exposed to disease every minute? You think I'd risk my life like this if I had some alternative? I'm dying all the time here. Now you show up 'cause you need something. Well, what do you need? *(He tries to speak: labored sound comes out. She doesn't get it. In frustration and anger he throws a chair. She cowers.)*

What'dya want? *(He indicates: pencil to write.)*

What? Pencil? *(She scrambles for it, gives it to him with a large piece of paper, the back of a form letter. He prints on it, painfully, then folds the paper as it had been folded and gives it back to her. She tears it open and reads.)*

"Goodbye Doreen"? Is that it? *(Yes. She drops her lipstick. He picks it up suddenly and offers it to her. She seems afraid to accept it, afraid to touch him. As she accepts it, however, a tenderness is transmitted. Her fingers touch his and memory is awakened.)*

Well, goodbye! *(She shrugs and sits. He moves to the door.)*

Wait! *(She's forgotten that he can't hear. His back is to her. She jumps up.)*

Wait! *(She taps his shoulder. He turns. They embrace.)*

Oh my God! *(He holds her tightly to him, then pushes her gently away to look at her. He touches her face, smiles, then with his thumb he gently closes each of her eyes, kisses them, then her lips. He puts on his scarf, his hat, turns and closes the door behind him. She turns, embraces herself, moves to the dressing table. Caught between memories of love and fear of death, she wipes his kiss from her mouth and as if in a trance, she starts, once again, to brush her hair.)*

END

RULES OF LOVE

CHARACTERS

PRIEST (Father Jim McGrath) — thirty or over.

WOMAN (Maisie) — thirty-five or over, a good-looking woman, dressed as if she is going on vacation.

SETTING

A confessional booth.

RULES OF LOVE

Father Jim McGrath, a Roman Catholic priest, walks to midstage, turns his back to the audience, genuflects, then walks to a chair. He sits, partially facing the audience, in what would be a confessional booth in a church. He's wearing a cassock, the long black gown that a priest often wears. Underneath, he wears trousers, socks, and shoes, all black, and a white tee shirt. He places a lavender or purple stole to hang from his neck like an open necktie — it's just a purple satin ribbon about two inches wide and a yard or so long. The priest and penitent are separated by a wall with a sliding door which he opens to talk to the confessing person. Even with this sliding door open, there is a metal screen between the two, and over the screen a black piece of silk to insure anonymity. So, the priest would face forward, at most just cocking his ear toward the voice of the penitent. On stage the whole setup may be represented simply by a chair with a back, in which the priest sits sideways, so that the penitent may use the back of his chair as a priedieu. Maisie kneels on a red velvet pad. The actors' behavior will indicate that they are enclosed and cannot see one another. She may talk to his face now and then, figuring out its whereabouts in the dark, but the priest keeps his profile to her, never risking to identify her, or any penitent, for this would violate the penitent's rights.

Maisie walks on, her footsteps echoing toward the would-be booth. She carries a suitcase which she leaves outside the area of confession. Cautiously, she steps inside and kneels. She is about to speak into his ear. He blesses her with his right hand, making a cross in the air. He does this blindly, then urges her to pronounce the opening words.

PRIEST. Bless me Father ...

WOMAN. Bless me Father for I have sinned. My last confession was two years ago.

PRIEST. Speak louder please?

WOMAN. My last confession was two years ago.

PRIEST. Okay. Two years ago. *(Silence.)* Are you there?

WOMAN. I'm here. I was ... afraid at first ...

PRIEST. Did you say afraid? I'm sorry, once again I can't ...

WOMAN. I said I was afraid, but ...

PRIEST. What are you afraid of?

WOMAN. I have committed a very grave sin, Father.

PRIEST. Alright.

WOMAN. And by afraid, I meant simply that I was nervous about coming here.

PRIEST. I'm not going to hurt you.

WOMAN. I know.

PRIEST. So take your time. *(Silence.)* Uh ... now, your sins?

WOMAN. I ... I've fallen in love.

PRIEST. That's no sin.

WOMAN. With a priest.

PRIEST. Uh.... Even so, that's no sin per se.

WOMAN. We've had sex fifteen, maybe twenty times.

PRIEST. Oh ... *(Now he recognizes the voice.)* Let me explain something: after a person confesses a sexual sin to a priest, if that priest follows up with an intimate act with that person, the priest cannot be forgiven except by the Pope. It's called solicitation.

WOMAN. I know about that.

PRIEST. But ... it ends the relationship. Don't you understand? And it ties his hands because he can't ... stop you from doing something foolish. *For God's sake! Find another priest to confess to!*

WOMAN. There are no other priests hearing confessions tonight.

PRIEST. Well, come back tomorrow.

WOMAN. I want to confess to you, Father. I know what I'm doing.

PRIEST.   Alright. Say what you want to say.

WOMAN.   At times I feel absolutely no guilt whatever for this relationship. I have the purest memories. Other times, the whole thing's a bummer. Every morning I wake up hating myself. I feel dirty.

PRIEST.   You shouldn't.

WOMAN.   Convince me.

PRIEST.   *(Shifts uncomfortably.)* Do you have any other sins to confess?

WOMAN.   Yes, sins against myself. Selling myself cheap. I don't mean literally, although sometimes I did feel like a piece of meat.

PRIEST.   Don't say that.

WOMAN.   Why else would I come here if I didn't feel that way? God, if there's one true sin that I should confess, it's the fact that I tried with all my power to get him to leave the priesthood.

PRIEST.   Easy ...

WOMAN.   If God hates me for that he has a perfect right to.

PRIEST.   There's no hate in God.

WOMAN.   Promise me that?

PRIEST.   Yes. I promise.

WOMAN.   I was alone for too long Father ...

PRIEST.   You don't have to ...

WOMAN.   ... and here was such a beautiful man worth caring for, and he wanted me. I did *not* go after *him*. I just couldn't resist his attention to me.

PRIEST.   Isn't that what most people yearn for?

WOMAN.   It was so damn egotistical.

PRIEST.   No it wasn't.

WOMAN.   I thought I could accomplish what God had failed to.

PRIEST.   And what was that?

WOMAN.   To get the guy off that ice-cold mountain he was sitting on all alone, like a lost little boy, afraid to love, afraid to touch.

PRIEST.   Maybe you succeeded.

WOMAN. I don't think so.

PRIEST. A person's changed for the rest of his life by such a thing.

WOMAN. What such a thing?

PRIEST. Love.

WOMAN. Well that's nice to hear.

PRIEST. Don't hurt this man. Maisie?

WOMAN. Don't use my name.

PRIEST. Don't punish him for his predicament. He suffers a lot because of his love for you. He needs your help.

WOMAN. That's why I came here.

PRIEST. How old are you?

WOMAN. Oh stop.

PRIEST. How old?

WOMAN. Thirty.

PRIEST. What took the woman so long to fall in love? Okay? What the hell was she doing before this? Eh? An attractive woman like you? Afraid of men, right? So you go after the least available guy, the least experienced? Hmmmn? Someone unmarried, but someone promised to God for the rest of his life?

WOMAN. I ... did not ... pursue you.

PRIEST. Bullshit. And one sexual conquest over this priest wasn't enough. You had to have twenty-seven.

WOMAN. Was it twenty-seven? I wasn't counting.

PRIEST. I was. And on top of that you wanted him for *life*. He's God's property.

WOMAN. I'm sure you'll never miss such a woman.

PRIEST. How dare you address me directly.

WOMAN. I don't have a church to hide behind.

PRIEST. Do you realize that I cannot give you absolution unless you're prepared to avoid the occasion in the future?

WOMAN. You mean avoid him?

PRIEST. Precisely.

WOMAN. I know the rules.

PRIEST. Well, shouldn't you *think* about this?

WOMAN. I ... got a job in another city. My plane leaves in a couple of hours.

PRIEST. *(Shocked.)* I see. Alright then. Do you have any other sins you wish to place before God?

WOMAN. You're really not going to stand up and fight for me?

PRIEST. What the hell do you mean?

WOMAN. You're not going to throw over all these cockamamie regulations and grab me and take the both of us out of here?

PRIEST. Shut up. You can't do this.

WOMAN. We can do whatever we want! What do *you* want to do?

PRIEST. *(Formal.)* Do you have any other sins you wish to place before God?

WOMAN. Shit. I've told you all my sins.

PRIEST. Then, for you penance, please attend Mass and offer it up for the spiritual welfare of this priest, and of yourself.

WOMAN. He needs it more than I.

PRIEST. Think of the years I worked to be what I am and you expect me to flush this down the drain in a minute? For what? And don't say love. I became a priest for love.

WOMAN. Bullcrap.

PRIEST. Every day's an act of love for me. Many others depend on me.

WOMAN. I was one of many?

PRIEST. Yes. In a manner of speaking. In another sense.... You meant more to me than the whole ...

WOMAN. The whole what? Jim?

PRIEST. The whole ... lot of them.

WOMAN. Oh Jim ...

PRIEST. Don't *call* me that in here.

WOMAN. Do you want me to move away?

PRIEST. I can't answer that in here. The minute you stepped in here everything changed for us. I don't know what I think. Please ...

WOMAN. Do you love me?

PRIEST. God, yes I do. Of course, but I can't help us now.

You've destroyed everything beyond your realization. You *ended* it. It's terrible what you did, Maisie. *(Pause.)*

WOMAN. It's terrible what you did.

PRIEST. For your penance go to Mass and offer it up for the welfare of this priest.... You might remember him often that way.

WOMAN. I will remember him often. I promise you that.

PRIEST. Thank you ...

WOMAN. Thank you, Father ...

PRIEST. You're welcome.

WOMAN. Goodbye, Father.

PRIEST. Now recite your Act of Contrition. *(He raises his hand, whispering the words of absolution in the old Latin form, overlapping he Act of Contrition.) Ego te absolvo ab omnibus censuris et peccatis, in nomine patis et filio et spiritus Sancti.... Amen.*

WOMAN. Oh my God I am heartily sorry for having offended Thee, and I confess all my sins because I dread the loss of heaven and the pains of hell. But most of all, because they offend Thee, my God, who art all good and deserving of all my love.... I firmly resolve, with the help of Thy grace, to confess my sins, do penance, and to amend my life. Amen. *(She stands up and leaves the confessional booth. She lifts her suitcase as if to exit church. The Priest steps out of the booth, calling out in a loud voice.)*

PRIEST. Which city? *(The Woman says nothing, but turns to continue on her way. Angrily, loudly, he cries out to her.)* Which city?

WOMAN. *(Smiling.)* Chicago. *(Exit. Lights fade on the Priest.)*

END

LENTEN PUDDING

CHARACTERS

ENCY — sixty, craggy, aproned, rural, yet intelligence and breeding are apparent.

MEGAN — fortyish, richly dressed, wearing a diamond ring and an expensive fur coat.

SETTING

Somewhere in the countryside.

LENTEN PUDDING

Aunt and niece are on a porch or deck against an old country house on a cold spring day. Water hoses, some terra cotta pots and gardening tools are about.

ENCY.   I just was not ... strong enough to make thirty-six Lenten puddings this year. The mailing became too expensive and some of you don't even send thank yous.

MEGAN.   Then why do you refuse to give us the recipe?

ENCY.   The recipe'll go to the grave with me.

MEGAN.   You just can't keep that recipe secret any longer. Now I drove eighty miles today. I tried to make one by guesswork last week. It didn't last three days.

ENCY.   All eaten?

MEGAN.   No. It went rancid. Tasted like rotten oranges baked in rubber. Then rigor mortis set in. I don't know why my mother never learned to make them. How could you two have been sisters?

ENCY.   It always beat me. My Lenten puddings last over five years in the refrigerator.

MEGAN.   Well, I poured rum all over my *stone.* It did soften ...

ENCY.   But tasted like fruit cake.

MEGAN.   God. Worse than fruit cake.

ENCY.   Rum is disgusting in Lenten pudding.

MEGAN.   How hostile of you to keep this secret from the entire family. I just want to pass my grandmother's recipe on to my daughter. Don't I deserve that?

ENCY.   You speak of deserving with that diamond ring you're wearing? You're drowning in your husband's greed. Like malformed kittens, you should all be put into a bag with a rock and thrown in Lake Babcock. And you drive eighty miles for the recipe you *deserve.*

MEGAN.   My grandmother's recipe.

ENCY.   Something money can't buy. *(Gleefully.)*

MEGAN.   This was my grandmother's summer house.

ENCY.   My *mother,* don't forget. And she was just like you. I never was particularly proud of her. Your mother was like her too. You were all hot-house bred. A fresh wind would wither you in seconds.

MEGAN.   I spent summers here as a child. Had you died before my mother this place would be mine.

ENCY.   So the old maid didn't deserve an inheritance? Which niece or nephew will she leave it to when she kicks off, as she seems to be ready to do? Are there rumors, Megan?

MEGAN.   No one wants this sad little place.

ENCY.   Just the recipe to Lenten puddings, because this is the first year one didn't arrive on every doorstep. For twenty years I cooked up in this shack from New Year's to Ash Wednesday, to keep warm, to put a pleasant smell in the house, to nourish the children of my brothers and sisters, because I'm the last of all the aunts and uncles. Thirty-six puddings take a whole winter, honey. This year I was too tired, and there was no goose this past Christmas.

MEGAN.   What on earth has the goose to do with it?

ENCY.   Wouldn't you love to know? Well … I beat them, the slavemasters, the Philistines and corporate barbarians. I hid out here but they'll get your little daughter with their TVs, their drugs and computers. It's the young they want to suck up. I survived without them up here. Now let the whole world go to hell.

MEGAN.   You should have married.

ENCY.   You think I don't know what love is?

MEGAN.   What has my poor daughter done to you? *You* never even met her.

ENCY.   How dangerous that would have been. Why was I punished by you all? Even though I presented you year after year with my penitential pies like a puppy begging to be forgiven. But no …

MEGAN.   You can't believe that *I* was punishing you. Why, I …

ENCY.   It's too late now to melt me. There'll be no thaw for Aunt Ency this spring. Oh, just go and leave me my privacy.

MEGAN.   Aunt Ency ... *(She rises.)* Be happy, darling. I'll go if you like.

ENCY.   Enjoy your drive.

MEGAN.   *(Walks to door to exit, then pauses, looking out.)* When I was a girl, this property seemed a continent. It's so small now, such a tiny garden. What happened to the cedar gazebo?

ENCY.   Wisteria pulled that down twenty years ago.

MEGAN.   A little house that let in the sun and the rain. I ... remember that ... maid loved to set in there behind the drooping purple blossoms, hiding from her work. Was she Russian?

ENCY.   We never had a maid.

MEGAN.   She'd sit inside the gazebo on that yellow wicker chair of Uncle Edward's. What happened to that chair?

ENCY.   You passed it on the porch on your way in.

MEGAN.   That tiny green thing on the porch?

ENCY.   It was yellow. I painted it white. Was white twenty years. Now it's green.

MEGAN.   Did the oaks stop growing?

ENCY.   Unlike chairs, trees grow. The oaks grew with you. That's all, Megan.

MEGAN.   So the trees remained my friends.

ENCY.   It *was* wisteria that pulled down your cherished gazebo ...

MEGAN.   They shared a fate, the gazebo and the wisteria. It was inevitable. Like marriage.

ENCY.   A form of strangulation I wouldn't know about.

MEGAN.   I remember the Russian sitting there resting, fanning herself with her blue apron, hiding behind the purple blossoms. How they drooped sadly, blooming all around her.

ENCY.   Pauline was never sad, nor did she ever hide from her work.

MEGAN.   She'd be sweating in her black woolen stockings, so tight around her legs. She'd roll them up with rubber bands and keep them so tight above her knees I worried about her circulation. Such white skin and black hair and blue eyes.

ENCY. You do remember her.

MEGAN. There's such sadness in foliage that hangs. Charles wouldn't allow willows on our property.

ENCY. Your grandmother planted those willows and when her sister, Aunt Margaret, came, she'd say for land's sakes plant trees that'll hold up their heads like this child of yours ...

MEGAN. Who was the child?

ENCY. I was the child.

MEGAN. You were your aunt's favorite?

ENCY. Yes. She was an old maid. She taught me the recipe for those Lenten pies. Not your grandmother. Your grand-mother had a cook. Your mother learned to cook from a poor Scots woman.

MEGAN. I missed my legacy entirely, didn't I?

ENCY. The Lenten puddings never *were* your legacy.

MEGAN. I must have broken fences when I followed you about up here, adoringly, everywhere. That was my downfall, wasn't it, following you about?

ENCY. Say what you mean.

MEGAN. What I saw that day in the gazebo. You thought I told the family about it, and I never had the courage to as-sure you that I wouldn't. I didn't tell a soul, I didn't breathe.

ENCY. They all found out about it anyway.

MEGAN. Not from me. I swear it to you. Aunt Ency, I was so afraid for you.

ENCY. Were you?

MEGAN. What happened to Pauline?

ENCY. She lives nearby, with her husband. Her children are grown.

MEGAN. You see her.

ENCY. She comes to clean twice a week.

MEGAN. She still cleans this house?

ENCY. She dusts while I make her lunch. We don't charge each other.

MEGAN. I imagine she has a great deal of love for you.

ENCY. We have kept faithful in our ways.

MEGAN. I envy her.

ENCY. Do you?

MEGAN.   I think you are a very strong, very beautiful woman to have as that close a friend. I hoped I had taken after you. But ... *(She buttons up her fur coat.)* Obviously I wasn't that lucky.

ENCY.   Who are we? We think we know in one decade, then it passes and we're asking the question again.

MEGAN.   If you become worse, I mean ill, would Pauline take care of you?

ENCY.   Yes, she would. Pauline will always be here.

MEGAN.   Well, then ... *(She starts to exit.)*

ENCY.   Here! Sit down before you run out of here. *(Megan sits. Ency gives up the recipe as she looks bitterly into her future.)* Her pudding. One tablespoon of goose fat. *(Pause.)* One orange rind, *(Pause.)* one cup Cognac ... *(Megan pulls pad and pencil out of her bag and begins to write furiously as lights fade.)*

END

TEN-DOLLAR DRINKS

CHARACTERS

STAR — thirty or over.

BETE — thirty or over.

Star is extremely well dressed, Bete, less so.

SETTING

A drinks table at the Russian Tea Room.

TEN-DOLLAR DRINKS

STAR.   I mean *everyone* was there. Everyone.

BETE.   The only stars I give a damn about are the ones on my kid's report card.

STAR.   How is he ... uh ...

BETE.   You forgot his name.

STAR.   Jesse.

BETE.   You forgot before you remembered. Just the way you saw me that night at Allison's, and lousy actress that you are you screwed up pretending not to see me.

STAR.   I saw you at Allison's.

BETE.   You are the worst.

STAR.   I was surrounded by twenty sycophantic moving mouths.

BETE.   Congratulations! Congratulations! But meantime we waited on your leash for you to say hi ...

STAR.   I had another party to go to.

BETE.   We figured as much my dear, but we refused to suffer the ignominy of you leaving first and waving us a pathetic *"Dear, what can I do?"*

STAR.   Talk about your son. That calms you.

BETE.   He got into Trinity.

STAR.   I presume that's good news.

BETE.   In my world it is.

STAR.   Well, that's nice.

BETE.   Till my money runs out. And don't you interpret that as I got you here to ask for a handout.

STAR.   Thanks. Here's to Jesse.

BETE.   That I'll drink to.

STAR.   Why'd you pick a place where the drinks are ten bucks?

BETE.   Me, invite a star to a no-class joint?

STAR.   I'll pick up the check if you let me.

BETE.   You bet your sweet ass I'll let you.

STAR.   What about all that voice-over work?

BETE.   New producer, new voice. Yesterday I got a call for a denture spot.

STAR.   You didn't.

BETE.   Old people are getting younger every day, honey.

STAR.   In LA they said you're up for that Pinter thing.

BETE.   Yeah.

STAR.   Tired?

BETE.   Just pissed. At my husband for being a drunk, my parents for dying, the dying was bad enough but leaving me shit ...

STAR.   Uh.... What the hell time is it?

BETE.   Now tell me you've got to go.

STAR.   No, go on ... your husband?

BETE.   I went and fell in love with an actor who hates himself, what else is new, except this one's a drunk so I go ahead and have his kid.

STAR.   You're talkin' about your son now.

BETE.   A terrific kid, knock wood.

STAR.   Does he see his dad?

BETE.   From a cab a couple weeks ago we saw him in rotted jogging shoes with glassy eyes, walking his dog.

STAR.   I thought he got himself a soap.

BETE.   He's on the "World" thing or "The Bold and the Broken."

STAR.   Then he should help with Jesse.

BETE.   He sends some money. *(Star stares as if to ask, "Then why kvetch?")*

STAR.   I hate to say this, but I got a damn P.R. meeting. So ... what is it? I showed up. So?

BETE.   Okay. I'm not jealous of you.

STAR.   That's it?

BETE.   Before we drift apart, as we obviously will, and you decide you don't know me at all anymore, I want in the record that I'll never envy you no matter what you accumulate, acquire ...

STAR. You've got too much on the ball to envy anybody.

BETE. True.

STAR. Too bad the rest of the world hasn't acknowledged this.

BETE. That's okay ... *(The insult catches up to her.)* Let's keep it between you and me shall we? *(Now letting it show.)* I'm not ashamed to look you in the eye and show you the hurt I feel.

STAR. Hurt for yourself or me?

BETE. Hurt that you walk around this town like you never knew a lot of your old friends.

STAR. Oh, Jesus.

BETE. Oh, Jesus, huh?

STAR. I win that cursed thing and suddenly I need four telephones and still I have to hire someone around the apartment to screen my callers. I hear from high-school friends, relatives I never met. I'm a freak. I'm worn out ...

BETE. We acted in the same company for ten years. We ate more dinners, spent more rotten hours together. I paid for more coffees. We slept together more nights ...

STAR. You're not going around claiming that.

BETE. You dog. I meant I had to put you to sleep, you drunk, on my couch a half dozen times. I'm not claiming to be your sister or some high-school jerk. You always were using everyone, everything. And it worked. What are you complaining about? So here's to your fucking obese ego, your obscene Oscar and your fame. *(Star pushes her drink.)*

STAR. You know what fame is? Multiply all the people you don't wanna know by two hundred million. That's fame. Fame ... is the drink that comes to your table from that dark corner of the restaurant and it could be from either a deranged stalker or your future lover. Either way if you don't drink the shit they'll hate you till they die. There is nothing spiritual about fame. Fame is prostitution without body contact. I know only one person who believed she was a true goddess. She refused to go to the bathroom because it would destroy her status and she wound up exploding in a Los Angeles emergency room. That's fame, Honey.

BETE. Well it didn't look that way at the Academy Awards.

STAR. *(With fear of the jealousy and the punishment.)* Did you watch?

BETE. You looked great. You said exactly the right thing. I was proud.

STAR. But did you watch?

BETE. Well, of course I watched.

STAR. Katie and Bill didn't watch. It's amazing how many didn't bother.

BETE. I can't believe Katie didn't watch it.

STAR. They had a gallery opening.

BETE. She saw it on the news, didn't she?

STAR. They saw nothing.

BETE. She didn't see the *paper*?

STAR. She said it wasn't delivered that day.

BETE. That bitch.

STAR. Well, nobody expected I'd get it, least of all me.

BETE. *I* didn't expect you to *get* it. You were up there with ancient deities, for heaven's sake.

STAR. Cut the bullshit.

BETE. Why? It's never for us to judge this stuff. So maybe you didn't deserve it ...

STAR. I didn't say I didn't deserve it. Oh you ...

BETE. I just hate you for going off into the sunset like some Wagnerian myth.

STAR. You're a better actress than I.

BETE. Just not as lucky as you. Is that the message?

STAR. You know you never were my best friend, for cryin' out loud.

BETE. But so unknown I deserved to be snubbed? You want me to buy that you don't know me at all? Ask me. I'll pretend we never met. Oh, you should be punished. God ...

STAR. Oh, c'mon. Hey.

BETE. It's like watching a ship sailing away forever.

STAR. For me it's like being *on* the ship.

BETE. I never had so close a friend win one of those horrid things.

STAR. Why don't you stop wasting time and tell me to my

face that you're jealous of me.

BETE.   What? I would despise myself if I felt one ounce … of … of jealousy of you of all people. I'm a damned good actress, better than most of the clowns out there.

STAR.   Including me.

BETE.   Yes, and you said it yourself. And I'd hate myself if I stooped to … to … jealousy … or …

STAR.   Then you hate yourself.

BETE.   You sonofabitch. I don't hate myself for having my son, for … for …

STAR.   Your son has nothing to do with this.

BETE.   I couldn't drag my ass around La-La Land with that kid.

STAR.   I didn't make it in LA. I made it here on the same stage, in the same company as you.

BETE.   *(Ping pong.)* I waited on tables. You've been subsidized since you were born.

STAR.   I worked my ass off.

BETE.   You're still not good enough.

STAR.   So why don't you throw your drink in my face? You've been dying to since you walked in here.

BETE.   Ach … throw my *drink?*

STAR.   Your hand's been shaking. You can hardly hold it back. Go ahead. Someone may take a picture. You'll get in the papers. People will gossip about it. You'll be welded to me for life. Maybe it'll get you a part in something.

BETE.   You weirdo.

STAR.   Oh, cut the shit. You're just as fucking hard-hearted an entrepreneur as I am. For a month you've been trying to provoke this argument. I'm here. I showed up. So go prove to the world you're intimate with a star …

BETE.   You know what a star is? You piece of shit? A star is one of those gorgeous goddamn glittering things in the heavens that mankind has been staring at for millions of years. It's a fucking *sun,* a giant, burning, eternal glory that gives more life than all our little fat heads put together cannot imagine. The kind of star you are is the paper kind, with glue on the back, the kind you buy by the hundreds in a little box for a buck.

STAR.   Cut the monologue and throw the fuckin' drink in my face. *(Bete stands in horror.)*

BETE.   I'm getting out of here, you crazy sonofabitch.

STAR.   Sure, because I'm wise to you. You aren't jealous, merely jealous. You're the same predatory opportunist you always were. You played your last card to get me here and you won. I'm bending to you, paying my dues so you can cut yourself in for your share of the pie. Well, take your share. Throw the goddamn drink. Throw the glass. *(Bete lifts her drink and flings it into Star's face. The two continue to look at one another. Bete starts to leave.)* Come back. Sit. Sit down. *(Bete sits slowly, totally emptied of feeling. Star grabs her hand and puts it to her cheek. She kisses Bete's hand gratefully, as Bete looks on, amazed and stunned.)*

END

FROZEN DOG

CHARACTERS

VINNY — around forty.
KEVIN — around forty.

SETTING

A room in a Catholic rectory.

FROZEN DOG

*Vinny and Kevin are two Catholic priests in Vinny's room
in the rectory of Saint Camilla's Parish. They've had a terrible fight. Kevin had just revealed that over the past ten
years, he'd been secretly writing the Bishop for permission to
be stationed wherever Vinny was stationed. This infuriated
Vinny, who feels now that Kevin had prevented his being stationed with his real pals in the priesthood. Also, the friend-
ship that did develop over the ten years has just been spoiled
by Kevin's disgusting admission. Vinny finds the intimacy
between him and Kevin revolting now, because it developed
artificially. It doubly irritates Vinny because he is at that
stage in his life where he feels he has given up too much.*

VINNY.   I ... I only meant to throw the drink in your face.
The glass simply flew out of my hand.
KEVIN.   Don't touch it. *(His head bump.)*
VINNY.   Just take your hand off it, stupid. *(He pulls Kevin's
hand away from his forehead and looks at the cut.)* Shit.
KEVIN.   Leggo.
VINNY.   You don't need stitches.
KEVIN.   Let me go back to my room.
VINNY.   The glass was wet ... I'm sorry.
KEVIN.   Well, there goes ten years down the drain.
VINNY.   What good are ten years together, with me, think-
ing it was a coincidence ... and all the while you were request-
ing it in those sneaky letters to the bishop. What must he
think we *are* to one another?
KEVIN.   That's what you're upset about? Your masculine im-
age?
VINNY.   No, God blast it. My autonomy. I'd like to have cho-
sen whom I was to be stationed with. I would have chosen
Corrigan. He was my best friend in the seminary, not you.

KEVIN.   Corrigan jumped the league and got married, Vinny.

VINNY.   Whatever. You had a choice. I had nothing.

KEVIN.   *(Hurt by that.)* That's nice. Ten years ago you should've written and asked to be with Corrigan. What can I tell you?

VINNY.   It's supposed to be God's will, I thought, whom you're stationed with.

KEVIN.   I'll be replaced soon and God's will can be done. I'm sorry.

VINNY.   When are you leaving?

KEVIN.   I mailed my letter to the bishop just before I came in here, so figure a couple weeks. I don't know.

VINNY.   Whom did you request to be with this time?

KEVIN.   The bishop offered me a job in the chancery.

VINNY.   Oh. Here comes the light. Now I see it. Just satisfy me with something before you walk out of here. What possessed you all these years to trail me, you sonofabitch?

KEVIN.   I told you. I was ... stuck on you. I ...

VINNY.   There must be another way to describe that.

KEVIN.   From the first day I saw you in the seminary.

VINNY.   Don't make me sick now.

KEVIN.   Oh, cut it out. When they locked those oak doors on three hundred kids on the edge of the damn Niagara River with nothing but a bunch of theology books and a pool table and twenty feet of snow outside, no mothers, fathers, girlfriends ... what did you expect would happen?

VINNY.   Wha ... what happened?

KEVIN.   Eyes. Eyes looking, glancin'. Minds crisscrossing across the room to one another, as if we were searching for our ... our special ...

VINNY.   *(Really angry at the implication here.)* Our special whats? *(Kevin doesn't dare answer.)* Our special *whats? (Still no answer.)* *You* made the mistake of becoming a priest, buddy, not me.

KEVIN.   Sure. I just never developed your capacity for keeping one foot in and one foot out of dreamland. I'd give it all up now for a little son or daughter. *(Suddenly, Kevin rips sheets off Vinny's bed.)* Where have our seed fallen, yours and mine? Huh?

VINNY.   Have you gone crazy? We made choices. We gave things up.

KEVIN.   We gave things up? You walk down the middle aisle like you have a broomstick up your ass because you're *drunk*. Your cassock stinks. People don't come to you anymore. You fall asleep in front of the damn TV. What happened to the Vinny Moran that all the guys in Niagara would have followed into Hell? The best basketball player, the emcee at all the functions ... the story teller ...

VINNY.   Okay, so you made yourself a satellite around a dead planet. I didn't invite you ...

KEVIN.   You weren't dead in Smithtown.

VINNY.   Smithtown? What about Smithtown?

KEVIN.   Ginger Murray, I believe her name was. Your first year out? We all heard about her back at the sem. You were having a nervous breakdown because you were in *love*.

VINNY.   Who said that ... that I was having a ... a ...

KEVIN.   Was it a lie? I always wanted to ask.

VINNY.   Go put some ice on your forehead.

KEVIN.   You feel that bad about answering me?

VINNY.   I ... found myself, just, I guess, melting, just wanting to join with her. She was like half of me, waiting for me.... Of course, it scared the both of us and we ended it, but I wasn't having any nervous breakdown.

KEVIN.   You were heroic.

VINNY.   I was a coward. That's what haunts me in the mornings when I look out that window. *(A police siren in the distance.)* Now all my caring is for them, out there.

KEVIN.   Social workers can take care of that.

VINNY.   They can't administer sacraments. Or don't you believe in that stuff anymore?

KEVIN.   Oh. Today you believe in something. Last time I was in here your faith was on the rocks, or so you led me ...

VINNY.   So I had doubts. If it turns out to be all fake magic, I'd still be a priest, for the sake of the people.

KEVIN.   But what if the magician keeps tiring of his tricks?

VINNY.   I smell the devil in this room.

KEVIN.   Shall I play his advocate?

VINNY.   Go to your desk job.

KEVIN.   What would you do if they discovered Christ's bones? Eh, Vinny? I mean if there was archeological proof that He never ascended, beyond any doubt, and they found His body in some cave?

VINNY.   I'd say Vinny, you blew it big. I'd open my appointment book and see that Mrs. Rodriguez's son is getting beat up and raped daily at Riker's and I'd make believe the kid was my son and I'd go to Riker's and try to stop my son from hanging himself. Rest of the time, I'd sleep so I could be strong when the likes of you walk in on me.

KEVIN.   Well, thank God you can pretend that Rodriguez is your kid. Next time you've had a half bottle of booze, have Rodriguez come in here and stand you on your feet for Mass. Get him to hold your brains together with his bare hands when you're not so sure there's a God up there anymore to thank for anything.

VINNY.   You are sure?

KEVIN.   Oh, shut the fuck up.

VINNY.   So come in here and talk about what happened to God.

KEVIN.   I'm more real to me right now. Okay? What happened to me and to you is more real right now.

VINNY.   Whaddaya want me to do ... lie down and bare my ass to you, 'cause you're finally ready to admit you're a ... what you are?

KEVIN.   Spit out what you want to call me you sonofabitch or I'll put a fist right through that TV of yours.

VINNY.   You mean my face ... you'd love to. Go ahead try it. *(The challenge cools them.)* Being a priest doesn't make you different from all those queers out there ...

KEVIN.   You have no right to call me that.

VINNY.   Queer! Queer! You better start calling yourself it. And don't project those feelings onto me. I never got stuck on a man, and I couldn't if I tried.

KEVIN.   Unless his name happened to be Corrigan.

VINNY.   Oh there was nothing of that in my affinity to

Corrigan or any male, and I swear it. It's like you coming in here and asking me to do math problems. I hate math — not that math is bad. I'm just the wrong guy for math.

KEVIN.   Do you think I want to *sin* with you? To fondle you or something?

VINNY.   What do you want? Jesus. What do you want from me?

KEVIN.   To admit it.

VINNY.   Admit what?

KEVIN.   Us. What we were ... to one another ... after ten years. Haven't we become something?

VINNY.   Oh no. I'm not your mate, or whatever you're imagining. I don't feel what you feel. Believe me, Kevin, for your own good, and get on with your life in your job or wherever, but — no. You assumed too much. There was never anything of the heart here with me for you. I swear on Christ himself. *(Kevin crumbles, sits.)* I don't mean to hurt you, but I never cared in anything near that way. Honest. You're a nice guy, but ... no. *(Pause, a long reckoning on Kevin's part.)*

KEVIN.   I have no interest in living a long life.

VINNY.   Now where is that coming from?

KEVIN.   I don't have the energy.

VINNY.   In the seminary, why'd you pick on me when there were hundreds of other guys?

KEVIN.   You kept looking at me.

VINNY.   *I* kept looking at *you?*

KEVIN.   And one day at recreation, you grabbed one of those black capes from the community rack and you threw it at me. "Let's go for a walk and say the rosery," you said. "Okay, sure," I said, and we went out and made a mile of tracks in the snow and I wondered: Why'd he ask me, with all those guys standing around?

VINNY.   You must've been near the door.

KEVIN.   No. There was a look in you eye. Agggh ... just forget it.

VINNY.   *(A beat, a drop in the energy. Kevin remains with his back to Vinny.)* God, was there ever snow up there.

KEVIN.   I still get this dream every once in a while: those black capes making noise, snapping in the wind. Remember when we saw those eagles circling out over the woods?

VINNY. I saw eagles with Corrigan, I remember ...

KEVIN. What about the bus rides to the Indian reservation? Remember that old bus we painted all those colors?

VINNY. A giant parrot on wheels, that death trap. How old were we?

KEVIN. I was nineteen.

VINNY. Do you remember the rumors that they sacrificed a white dog up there?

KEVIN. Oh my God, I saw it. It was a chow, hangin' from his feet, and the assistant rector, whatzizname ... he stopped the bus and made us take the thing down. It was frozen — its legs frozen straight out. They stood it up, and it looked like it was howling to the sky.

VINNY. *(Suddenly remembering the name.)* Father Mirabelli.

KEVIN. Mirabelli. He jumped the league, you know. Got married.

VINNY. How come I never saw the dog?

KEVIN. You must've missed a week.

VINNY. Mirabelli. All the cream has left.

KEVIN. No. Every night during Vespers, at the Salve Regina, your face, Vinny.... It used to ... used to get all pale. I swear to you.

VINNY. Cut it out ...

KEVIN. Guys talked about it, how your eyes got when you looked up at the blue window at the blessed Virgin up there ...

VINNY. Yeah?

KEVIN. What were you seeing up there?

VINNY. How high up she was, how young and just a little pregnant, never touched by a man. She's the one made me safe, lookin' down at us from up there.

KEVIN. I'd kneel a couple pews behind you. You didn't see me, but I put in a lot of hours there with you.

VINNY. Was Christ really there with us?

KEVIN. I thought so.

VINNY. I swear I used to imagine his breathing. You'd go

in, genuflect and kneel down, and next thing would come that breathing noise.

KEVIN.   It was me breathing behind you.

VINNY.   That wasn't funny.

KEVIN.   Just a joke.

VINNY.   If I had left the priesthood, would you have followed me then?

KEVIN.   If you left the priesthood? Yes, I would have followed you.

VINNY.   Don't give me that, Kevin.

KEVIN.   I was in love with you, Vinny.

VINNY.   *Geeez.* Don't! I could stand you thinking the words, but I could kill you for sayin' them.

KEVIN.   Kill me.

VINNY.   Smithtown split me me in two and I had to choose, even though it made me hate God ... *(Blaming Kevin somehow.)*

KEVIN.   Whatever happened to her?

VINNY.   Huh? She married a cop.

KEVIN.   The two of you ever...?

VINNY.   Once. Once. *(Drifting.)* I could easily have gone off with her.

KEVIN.   Why didn't you?

VINNY.   *(Back to the subject.)* I'd have had to leave the priesthood, wouldn't I?

KEVIN.   Better than hating God.

VINNY.   *(Drifting again.)* Oh, I don't hate him anymore. I just miss him. *(Back to the subject.)* But you never had to split yourself, did you?

KEVIN.   Whattya mean?

VINNY.   You just wrote sneaky letters to the bishop, and he gave me to you on a silver platter like a stuffed pig.

KEVIN.   It wasn't that one sided.

VINNY.   I could reach out and slap you out of sheer jealousy of you getting your way ...

KEVIN.   Easy with the gestures.

VINNY.   ... and now you've decided to simply walk out of my yard after stealing all the figs from my tree ...

KEVIN. What figs?

VINNY. ... leaving me uncovered in the snow. *(He swings.)*

KEVIN. You're crazy.

VINNY. It's time for everyone to dump Vinny Moran.

KEVIN. I didn't dump you.

VINNY. The honeymoon's over, eh? *(Swings.)*

KEVIN. Calm down, Vinny.

VINNY. Well go, vampire. *(Swings.)*

KEVIN. Don't use that word with me.

VINNY. You sucked on my life.

KEVIN. I can use my hands, too.

VINNY. Outta my sight. *(Vinny lands on Kevin.)*

KEVIN. Don't tempt me, Vinny. I don't wanna hurt you.

VINNY. Faggot priest! *(He is powerful, moving in, slapping Kevin with each word.)* Go, faggot ... *(Slap.)*

KEVIN. You crazy ... sonofabitch.

VINNY. Go, faggot ... *(Slap.)*

KEVIN. Think. You're ... You're ...

VINNY. Faggot priest ...

KEVIN. I'm losin' it Vinny, and I swear I'll floor ya.

VINNY. *I don't want you. You hear?*

KEVIN. Fine.

VINNY. I want Corrigan, not you. *(He shakes Kevin.)*

KEVIN. Stop with the hands now.

VINNY. I don't want you.

KEVIN. Alright.

VINNY. I want Ginger ... I want the Virgin Mother in the blue window ...

KEVIN. Easy. *(Vinny's slaps are becoming ineffectual pawings.)*

VINNY. I want Christ on the cross. I want God in Heaven, but not you. Not you, Kevin ... Kevin ...

KEVIN. Hold on. *(Vinny is slipping down, out of breath, at the same time he is embracing Kevin, crushingly now, bringing him down with him to the floor.)*

VINNY. I'm freaking.

KEVIN. I gotcha Vin.

VINNY. Please.

KEVIN. What?

VINNY.   Don't leave me.
KEVIN.   You don't have to say anything.
VINNY.   Don't leave me here.
KEVIN.   Don't worry.
VINNY.   I wouldn't do it to you.
KEVIN.   I'll blow up the mailbox. Something. Don't worry.
VINNY.   I care. I ...
KEVIN.   Okay. Shut up.
VINNY.   ... in my own way ...
KEVIN.   You don't havta. Shhh.
VINNY.   You must know it.
KEVIN.   I know it.
VINNY.   I'd never do this to you.
KEVIN.   I'm not leaving.
VINNY.   Promise.
KEVIN.   I promise.
VINNY.   I'd never do it to you.
KEVIN.   Okay now shut up.
VINNY.   Never.
KEVIN.   Shhh.
VINNY.   I couldn't.
KEVIN.   Shhhh ...

END

SOFT DUDE

CHARACTERS

DOLL — anywhere between twenty and fifty.
DUDE — anywhere between twenty and fifty.

SETTING

Open with a bright and active *Goldberg Variation,** by Bach.

A shabby room with a little electric oven in a sorry hotel. The lighting does nothing to hide the squalor but as the characters become sympathetic, the lighting changes subtly, becoming richer, even enchanting. Bach's sweetest Variation plays.

*See Special Note on Songs and Recordings on copyright page.

SOFT DUDE

DOLL.   Guess what I saw last night. *The Wizard of Oz.* You know how I love chocolate pudding? Not even chocolate pudding was as good. On the big screen I mean, not on TV or anything, you know, a movie. I always dreamed of it on the big screen.... What are you doin'?

DUDE.   *(Scratching .)* Nothin'.

DOLL.   I thought you were touchin' yourself.

DUDE.   Na.

DOLL.   You want me to play with it?

DUDE.   *(Mischievously, because he knows she hates it.)* No. Hold my hand.

DOLL.   Whatch out, I'm warnin' ya. Listen to me. When that witch melts, it's such a ... relief. Stop scratchin'.

DUDE.   I'm itchy.

DOLL.   It ain't crabs, is it?

DUDE.   Maybe it is.

DOLL.   Only you can get the crabs by not having sex with anyone.

DUDE.   I had it with someone.

DOLL.   When?

DUDE.   This afternoon.

DOLL.   You can't screw me, but you can screw some girl?

DUDE.   I paid for it.

DOLL.   So pay me.

DUDE.   I don't wanna do it that way with you. *(Phone rings.)*

DOLL.   Yes. Yeah. Yeah, skip the formality, you read the ad and you want a massage ... $125 at my studio, $150 at your place. You can't come to my studio. Of course I'm pretty. You think I'd have the nerve to charge $150 if I wasn't exceptional? No. I work alone. What? *(To Dude.)* Hey, this guy wants a threesome. *(Dude declines.)* He'll pay us both.

DUDE.   I can't get no rekshun with you around.

DOLL.   So let him deal with that when the time comes. $250 bucks.

DUDE.   Na.

DOLL.   *(On Phone.)* Just me is all I can do. *(The caller hangs up, then she does.)* Up yours yourself with a giant cactus, creep. *(To Dude.)* What good are you? You make $250 a week. You can't get a hard on, and you're ugly as shit. How much you drop to get laid?

DUDE.   Fifty.

DOLL.   Fifty dollars? What was she, a centenarian? You used to drop a hundred a week on me before that thing went soft. Jesus, I thought you were some big shot. Now I can't get a rise outta you even if I paid you.

DUDE.   I want to, Doll. Honest to God.

DOLL.   No wonder you're impatient. You get laid and beat off all day while I'm workin'. Stupid me. I figured, ah, he's cute, he's got a nice little job, I coulda had some steady business from him and enjoyed it for once. Soon as I get interested ... zoom ... you turn into one of those rubber duckies with a whistle on the bottom: Fwee-Fwoo, Fwee-Fwoo. Now I'm makin' you feel better, right? Makin' fun of you helps, right?

DUDE.   No. You're just mad at me.

DOLL.   You hate me, so shouldn't I be mad?

DUDE.   No, Doll.

DOLL.   Well ya don't wanna get into me.

DUDE.   I want to.

DOLL.   You sit around here just to show me how disgusting you think I am.

DUDE.   No, Doll.

DOLL.   You don't even wanna screw me.

DUDE.   I want to.

DOLL.   You can't get it up is not wanting to. When someone don't turn you on no more, split. Gimme a light. I kiss you. I play with your tits. I go down of you, *(Puff.)* It's like you took ether or something. But you can do it fine with some other whore ... some cheap fifty-dollar cow and it's right up there. Fourth of July. 'Cause in your mind I'm shit, and now you sit in my chair loaded with crabs. Very nice.

DUDE.   I ain't got no crabs, fer Chrissake. I'm just itchy. The doc said from nerves.

DOLL.   What did the doctor tell you about your penis?

DUDE.   He said it was in my head.

DOLL.   That's where it's hidin' out? Good – good.

DUDE.   No.

DOLL.   Couldn't he give you any pills or something?

DUDE.   How old are you? Really, this time.

DOLL.   Twenty-four. Now you know.

DUDE.   Once you said thirty.

DOLL.   So I lied to you. I'm twenty-four. *(He smiles. She laughs.)* You know damn well I'm thirty.

DUDE.   So don't you want to get married someday?

DOLL.   What are you? Listen. Go. Split. My head's up to here.

DUDE.   Answer me. Why doncha?

DOLL.   I got a headache. So you think I'd be jerkin' off with you here ugly shit if I had someone nice who'd marry me? Hah? Go, get rid of yourself.

DUDE.   What're ya bein' ugly? Jus' 'cause I can't have sex I gotta split? I mean you meet someone at a party do you gotta get fucked from them before you talk to them?

DOLL.   Gimme a light.

DUDE.   So what're ya bein' ugly?

DOLL.   I feel ugly.

DUDE.   You shouldn't feel ugly, you're not ugly.

DOLL.   You make me feel ugly. You ugly shit.

DUDE.   Because I can't get a hard on?

DOLL.   Your chicken is burning. *(He jumps to toaster oven, opens it, and takes out his chicken.)*

DOLL.   Use the pot-holder.

DUDE.   No. You stay right there. It's just right. I know you get hungry around now. Are ya?

DOLL.   Medium. *(He puts out two dishes.)*

DUDE.   You have a corkscrew?

DOLL. Is that some suggestive joke?

DUDE. The wine.

DOLL. In the cabinet there.

DUDE. Stay where you are.

DOLL. Such a scene for a lousy chicken. We coulda called the Colonel. I'm not even hungry.

DUDE. If you'd stop smokin' for five minutes.... Come on. Sit here. *(He lights the candles.)*

DOLL. This is so stupid.

DUDE. What's stupid about it?

DOLL. With your luck the candles'll get soft and bend over and burn the goddamn table. Floop! *(Laughing at her own joke, she makes a gesture of the candles going limp. He stares down at the table and very slowly pushes one dish. It pushes the other. Soon, the chicken and everything falls to the floor.)* Wait! Whatcha do that for?

DUDE. Good-bye, Baby.

DOLL. No, wait. I'm sorry. Look, everything's okay. The floor's clean. Sit down. *(He sits.)* Plastic dishes are good for this. It's perfectly all right.

DUDE. Don't feel bad, but I gotta go now. Humpty Dumpty. Eh? That's what you did ...

DOLL. Huh?

DUDE. What I am. It's broken. You got nothing but a fuck or a suck to give. I can't get no hard on. And the stuff I got ... you don't want, my damn chicken, nothin'.

DOLL. You compare a chicken to a normal adult like fuck?

DUDE. It's the best I can do. Why is it so important to get fucked by me? You get it twenty times a day. You'll be gettin' fucked at eleven o'clock. Can't you eat somethin' with a friend without gettin' fucked for Crissakes? The thing died for us.

DOLL. A guy fucks me, I know what he wants and it's over with. You, I don't know what you want. You scare me. What do you want from me?

DUDE. Be nice to me.

DOLL. Be nice?

DUDE. And I'll be nice to you.

DOLL. And that's all?

DUDE.   What else is there?

DOLL.   I bump into this old lady in the hall, you know? So she's nice to me — and you know my friend Gloria with the hair — she's nice to me. My mother, right? *She* was nice to me. Who needs nice? Nice isn't all there is. I go for you, right?

DUDE.   You do?

DOLL.   You're nice. I go for you. I admit it. I desire to fuck you, you can't fuck nothin'. Now is that a very nice way to deal with me? Out there, people, they're nice. They have a drink, they talk, right? So it turns out you are no different than the old lady in the hall. If that's all you want to be, then hello nice lady, gimme a light. *(Puff.)* So we're gonna have dinner, let's eat for now. I got an engagement at eleven. Let's eat tonight and give each other a call every ten years or so to chat. And if we ever bump into each other on the street, we say hello. We'll be nice. C'mon. The floor's clean.

DUDE.   I'll see ya.

DOLL.   So it died for nothin'? It died for nothin'.

DUDE.   I'm not hungry.

DOLL.   You're gonna make me the guilty one.

DUDE.   Why should you feel guilty?

DOLL.   Because I made you feel bad.

DUDE.   What do you care if I feel bad?

DOLL.   I care. Maybe it's my fault. I'm the only one it happens with, your problem, right?

DUDE.   I had it before I met you.

DOLL.   But we had sex great for a couple months there.

DUDE.   If it's a hooker and I'm paying my way, I'm okay.

DOLL.   But I'm a whore, honey. What am I?

DUDE.   No ... not to me ... never. You're not a whore, you're ...

DOLL.   What? *(He looks at her, trying to form an answer.)*

DUDE.   I dunno.

DOLL.   Don't go.

DUDE.   You sure about this now, Doll?

DOLL.   Yeah ... stay and let's eat.... Gimme a match.... You don't mind eatin' wet chicken? Once I emptied a whole pot of spaghetti into the sink because I forgot the colander. It was delicious. And I got parsley. You like parsley? *(She grabs the jar of dried parsley.)*

DUDE.   I don't care.

DOLL.   Sit down. My mother ... parsley was her favorite vegetable. Eat it. I'm hungry now.

DUDE.   The chicken is good.

DOLL.   Maybe we should dump it on the floor every time. Hah?

DUDE.   Man, it's perfect.

DOLL.   My mother was a terrific cook, she used to cook five meals a night 'cause my brothers all liked different food. Them shitheads.

DUDE.   You had brothers?

DOLL.   Me, the only girl. It was Hell.

DUDE.   You probably got a lot of attention.

DOLL.   Yeah. They used to get me in the toilet and make me suck them — everything. And once my father caught my brother Louie forcin' me to go down and you know what he did? He beat the shit outta *me.* Can you believe that? And you know, for such horny pricks that they were, not one of my brothers got married except Johnny boy, and he was gay.

DUDE.   Are you sure?

DOLL.   He used to act like a girl, so you figure it out. My father despises him to this day. He goes back, the poor sucker, every Sunday with his skinny wife, if she ain't pregnant in her ninth month. Maybe Johnny boy ain't gay. Somebody's knockin' her up. My father likes the kids, specially the girl.

DUDE.   Do you go back on Sundays?

DOLL.   Me? Never. I got no use for him. No use for him, poor old ... agggh ... he's just an old man now. I'm free. No. I'm different. When my wings sprouted, boy did this little girl fly.

DUDE.   Me, too.

DOLL.   Oh yeah?

DUDE.   I flew, man did I fly.

DOLL.   You're not shittin' me or anything are you, Dude?

DUDE.   Whattyamean?

DOLL.   You content just tellin' stories and not jumpin' my

170

bones?

DUDE. Yeah. Really.

DOLL. I'll bet if you tried transcendental meditation ...

DUDE. Don't make such a big thing of it.

DOLL. You ever go home? Ya know, to your folks?

DUDE. They're dead.

DOLL. Lucky you.

DUDE. Naa. Sometimes I think I'd like to ... I dunno, talk to my ole lady.

DOLL. Your mother? You miss her?

DUDE. Yeah. She was real close, ya know what I mean? Used to tell me stories ya know? And I'd help her round the kitchen. I had a tomato farm.

DOLL. You a farm boy?

DUDE. Naaa. We lived in this building, not a tenement or anything, dignified ya know, middle class.

DOLL. Yeah ...

DUDE. But there was a fire escape and all ...

DOLL. Yeah yeah.

DUDE. And we had tomatoes in the pots out there.

DOLL. Whad ya know. On the fire escape?

DUDE. Yeah, on the fire escape. She liked nature, my mother, ya know?

DOLL. Ya mother sounds like a pretty normal, ya know, a sensitive woman.

DUDE. She was. But she took no shit from anyone.

DOLL. Oh yeah?

DUDE. Bet your ass. She spoke once, and God help you if she spoke the second time, you got the hot spoon on your legs.

DOLL. What hot spoon?

DUDE. From her cookin'. She'd turn and zap, your legs — you know, I wore short pants those days. She used to ... usta ... to.... What was I sayin'?

DOLL. The hot spoon.

DUDE. No. Oh yeah. The fire escape. She use to, she usta, to ...

DOLL. Yeah?

171

DUDE. Ya gonna laugh at me?

DOLL. Swear to God.

DUDE. She used to make me take off my clothes.

DOLL. What for?

DUDE. You know. I wouldn't go to school. Never. Hated school, so she took her spoon and made me strip down, to my birthday suit ...

DOLL. You're kiddin'.

DUDE. Bam with the spoon. My underwear, socks every stitch and she'd put me out on the fire escape.

DOLL. *(Outraged.)* Naked?

DUDE. *(Laughing.)* With the tomatoes.

DOLL. Dude, you gotta be kiddin'.

DUDE. Swear to God.

DOLL. But why?

DUDE. 'Cause I wouldn't go to school, I'm tellin' ya. And the people, Doll, swear you'll never repeat what I just told you. I never told a soul in the world.

DOLL. I swear on the holy blood of Jesus.

DUDE. The girls across the way right opposite, right? They laughed, right? She'd close the window and trap me out there till it got dark. Wouldn't you laugh: A bare-ass kid on the fire escape?

DOLL. I wouldn'ta laughed. I would not've laughed.

DUDE. You're a good woman, Doll.

DOLL. My God in Heaven, I would ... not have laughed. She was an animal, your mother.

DUDE. Naaa.

DOLL. How'd you let her get away with that?

DUDE. Hey, I wasn't seventeen or anything. I was a real, a kid, you know? She was somethin', though, a good fuckin' woman. Hey Doll, don't worry.

DOLL. I feel so fuckin' sorry for you.

DUDE. *(Takes her hand.)* Don't worry.

DOLL. My hands are too skinny. *(He won't let her extricate her hand.)* Don't hold my hand. *(She's warned him of this before.)*

DUDE. What's to hold hands?

DOLL. It's stupid. Not stupid. You know I don't ever let anybody touch my hands. Nobody. You know that.

DUDE.   Try it.

DOLL.   I don't go for it I told you, it's corny, now you gotta let go?

DUDE.   Please Doll ...

DOLL.   Let goa me.

DUDE.   Doll ...

DOLL.   Look, I said I'm sorry for ya, now let go, Dude.

DUDE.   Don't be ashamed.

DOLL.   Get out. You don't fool me.

DUDE.   Doll, what are ya sayin'?

DOLL.   Take your act to the Salvation Army.

DUDE.   I'm not foolin' ya, Doll, I'm not foolin' ya.

DOLL.   Get your filthy hands offa me.

DUDE.   You are a whore.

DOLL.   That's right. That's my job.

DUDE.   A goddamn shit-ass whore.

DOLL.   Now you're talkin' like yourself.

DUDE.   Gimme your hand.

DOLL.   Go fuck yourself. *(Dude takes bills from his pocket.)*

DUDE.   Hun'red twenty-five dollars ... I'm payin' ya to hold your disgusting hand, you greasy whore.

DOLL.   I'll take it. *(She holds out her hand. Dude takes it, pulls her close to him, cautiously, tenderly, they kiss.)*

END

WATCHMAN OF THE NIGHT

CHARACTERS

MIKE — wears the perfect gray film noir suit and fedora.

FARNSWORTH (voice over).

CELESTE (voice over).

NED — wears jeans and a tee shirt.

SETTING

A reporter's room in a city setting. The place has a film noir feeling.

WATCHMAN OF THE NIGHT

Mike, a newspaper reporter, enters his apartment, cigarette hanging from mouth, shirt open, tie pulled down, exhausted, carrying his late newspaper, his briefcase, and a six-pack of beer in a brown grocery store bag. He drops newspaper and briefcase as if unburdening himself of his whole life. He goes to his answering machine and punches the replay button. He opens a beer and drinks, as the tape rewinds with squealing foreshadows of messages. The tape stops. Silence. Then we hear the first beep.

Somewhere in Ned's long monologue both the sound and the lighting change, turning him from a distant caller to a presence on stage equally vivid to Mike's.

Beep.

FARNSWORTH.   *(Voice over.)* Mike? It's Farnsworth. Midnight. You probably went to your girl's place or some gin mill but I just read your copy and Jesus, this is the quality of writing I've been praying for for this damn newspaper. When more reporters like you hang around here till eleven to get it right, then not only this rag but this whole country will start falling back into place. It's exciting. I don't know how to repay you, pal ...
MIKE.   With a decent salary, you shit.
FARNSWORTH.   See ya at eight A.M., fella. *(Mike throws beer can at the machine. The next beep.)*
CELESTE.   *(Voice over.)* Mike, it's Celeste at 1:00 A.M. Are you crazy running out of here like that? All I said is I need some space. This isn't easy for me either. Call me when you get in. I'm worried. Don't let me wait up.

MIKE. Get lost. *(Beep. Voice change, tired.)*

CELESTE. Mike, it's one-thirty and I know you're there. I'm worried about you. Are you there?

MIKE. Go to bed.

CELESTE. Michael. Pick up 'cause I won't hang up. You want me to run your tape out? I will. Maybe you're at some bar. I'll wait one more half hour. If you don't call me by then, I'll know what you're trying to tell me.

MIKE. Go to bed for cryin' out loud.

CELESTE. *(Beep — dragging voice.)* Mike it's 2:00 A.M. and I'm not thrilled with this. Michael ... don't make me feel guilty. Please call. Call. I'll wait up all night.

MIKE. Wait all your life, baby. *(Gives the machine the finger. Beep.)*

CELESTE. Mike, it's 2:00 A.M. and I'm not thrilled with this. I know you're there. Are you there? Mike, don't make me worry. Now call. You hear?

MIKE. Sure baby. *(Finger. Beep.)*

CELESTE. You wanna finish off this way, fine. I'm not going to be the guilty one. I'm going to bed and putting my machine on, okay? If I don't hear from you, well, I'll assume we're dead.

MIKE. Fool. *(He gets up to turn off the machine and just as he is about to, the telephone rings in the room: once, twice, then the beep sounds and a male voice speaks softly and poetically, amplified through the machine speaker. Juke box dance music is thumping in the background.)*

NED. This is the "watchman of the night." It's 3 A.M. Are you there? "In the real dark night of the soul it's always 3 A.M." F. Scott Fitzgerald said. Hey Dave, pick up. C'mon, don't let the beep cut us off. Take your hand away and breathe, you sonofabitch. You hear that music in the background? It's the music of Hell. I'm at the port of entry with two hundred faceless orphans and we're drowning in dance and drink and terror 'cause it's easier than going home to our zero lives. David. Answer. "He's whining again." Isn't that what you're thinking? Big Dave wouldn't sink to that. Dave's a real he-man. Where's the beep? You fuck. When I heal from what you've done to me, I'll probably be turned to stone just like you. The whining you hear mother fucker? — It's because I'm alive and tender and I hurt, and I'm proud of it. You can't hurt. Not while you're wearing a $2000 suit. You can only pray that someone like me will kill himself over you so you can own his gift of love with no responsibility. But remember, I was the one who was happily married. You fell on your knees in my kitchen and begged me, 'cause only I could save you. "Just be my friend. Nothing sexual. No, no. Just dare to see me without turning away, stay with my eyes, just dare, touch fingers." And I ... I did. I felt what you wanted me to feel. It was strange and beautiful. I admitted it. And I got scared, and I cried. And you jumped up and held onto me and you said, "Don't be afraid of what's human. I'll never let you go, never. I'll hold you up forever." What happened to forever, Dave? Huh? What the fuck happened to *forever*? You like, you made me dig up a grave ... and exhume such ... feelings, my father, my brothers, feelings I had buried when I was a kid, and when you swore to stick with me, well, I just lifted the cadaver, stood it on its feet and it blinked. It moved. It spoke. It said: "You can love a man. You can." But when this monster got healthy, it scared Big Dave and now Big Dave won't talk to me, but I know he's listening, hiding in the shadows, praying that I'll disappear. Well I will. I'll answer your prayers tonight. Gonna lead my monster back to its grave, shoot it in the brain, and cover it up forever ...

MIKE.   (*Grabbing up the telephone and shouting into it.*) Don't shoot your monster. Do you hear me? (*Lights go out on Ned. His voice is heard on the answering machine.*)

NED.   Who.... Who is this?

MIKE.   My name's Mike.

NED.   Mike who?

MIKE.   You dialed 555-9664.

NED.   I dialed 9644.

MIKE.   9664.

NED.   Why'd you let me go on?

MIKE.   Look, I'm straight but I have the same monster. My girl threw me out tonight.

NED. I'm sorry.

MIKE. I'm sorry about this bastard Dave.

NED. It's okay.

MIKE. It stinks, man. Look. You've got my number now. I'm available. I mean, not for ... not for ... any monkey business, I mean a drink, a talk.... Hello?

NED. "Monkey business"? What's that?

MIKE. I mean.... Look, you got a drink in your hand?

NED. Yeah.

MIKE. Wanna toast?

NED. Toast what?

MIKE. Our monsters. Yours and mine. Should we?

NED. I don't know.

MIKE. Let's go. Lift your glass. *("CLICK!!!)* Hello? You there? Hello? *(Dial tone.)* What did I say? What did I say?

END

UNCLE CHICK

CHARACTERS

CHICK — is in his late forties.

BRIAN — is twenty four.

SETTING

An apartment in a tenement building in Greenwich Village, New York City.

UNCLE CHICK

At rise Chick is packing cartons, going through old letters.
Brian is softly knocking at the partly opened apartment door.
There's a suitcase and tied cartons on the floor.

BRIAN. *(Enters.)* Uncle Chick.

CHICK. Brian. What the hell you doin' here?

BRIAN. I came to visit you.

CHICK. *(Stuffs letters into a carton and goes to door to greet Brian.)* Just like that you came … at midnight?

BRIAN. I was down here.

CHICK. Your father know?

BRIAN. I don't live home anymore, Uncle Chick.

CHICK. Down here doin' what?

BRIAN. I bought coffee, from the Greek place downstairs. *(Brian opens the bag, takes out Chick's coffee.)* This is for me. *(Hands Chick a container of coffee and moves past him into the apartment.)* Nice apartment. What's in the boxes?

CHICK. Books, records …

BRIAN. *The Savage Hunters of the Labrador Peninsula,* by Frank Speck?

CHICK. Take it with you.

BRIAN. Is it interesting?

CHICK. It's not my book.

BRIAN. Then how can you give it to me?

CHICK. Brian.

BRIAN. What's the story? You moving?

CHICK. They belonged to somebody else.

BRIAN. Who?

CHICK. How's my brother?

BRIAN. Fine. Uncle Mike's rackin' up bucks in the music

business, man. Records, cassettes, you know? He goes to Dublin, London to present stuff. Somethin'. And Aunt Rosemary won a trip to Hawaii.

CHICK. When's she goin'?

BRIAN. When could you get Aunt Rosemary to leave Passaic?

CHICK. What's gonna happen to the ticket?

BRIAN. She gave it back to the nuns. They're gonna raffle it all over again.

CHICK. How *you* doin'?

BRIAN. How do I look?

CHICK. Older. How'd you find me, Brian?

BRIAN. Tonight I was with this guy.

CHICK. Yeah?

BRIAN. Says he knows you.

CHICK. Who?

BRIAN. A Steve?

CHICK. I know a hundred Steves.

BRIAN. An architect from Tribeca?

CHICK. Oh. That asshole.

BRIAN. Is he? I don't ...

CHICK. How'd you run into him?

BRIAN. At Uncle Charlie's.

CHICK. In Passaic?

BRIAN. No. The *bar* ... Uncle Charlie's.

CHICK. A gay bar? Shit.

BRIAN. *(Brian smiles, shrugs.)* It was good enough for you.

CHICK. It was not good enough for me. I never stepped foot into one of those pits.

BRIAN. Okay. Tell me where should I go?

CHICK. If you had any sense you'd go back to New Jersey.

BRIAN. You want me to be a hockey star like my brother? Get my face bashed in.

CHICK. I don't interfere with my brother's kids.

BRIAN. You're supposed to interfere with me. I'm your godchild. Remember? You're supposed to take care of my soul.

CHICK. You got a job?

BRIAN. Pastry chef. Got my own apartment.

CHICK.   Where?

BRIAN.   Hell's Kitchen. Eleventh Avenue.

CHICK.   Jesus.

BRIAN.   I'm okay there. So how ... what was it with you and this architect?

CHICK.   Did you do anything with that scum bag?

BRIAN.   I don't use my mouth for anything except talk. And after ... I say toodle-oo.

CHICK.   When did you come out?

BRIAN.   I was about six or seven.

CHICK.   Six or seven?

BRIAN.   You took me in the ocean on your shoulders. I had two fists of your hair like this, and baby you had hair down to here 'cause it was the seventies. Granma was alive and you took us. You taught me to eat clams on the half shell that day.

CHICK.   You spit them all out.

BRIAN.   I didn't swallow them but I liked them.

CHICK.   No. This is bad, Brian.

BRIAN.   I came to visit you.

CHICK.   You *call* people first.

BRIAN.   You wouldn'ta let me up.

CHICK.   You're here. What do you want?

BRIAN.   To look at ya ...

CHICK.   And what d'ya see?

BRIAN.   I see my father's brother, 'cept you're much cuter than him.

CHICK.   Don't assume you can talk any way you like here.

BRIAN.   I wondered who these women were you used to sleep with.

CHICK.   What women?

BRIAN.   Aunt Madeline use to say. "When's he gettin' married that Chick?" And my father'd tell her "Chick's's a jigalo. He's got a hundred girlfriends," I imagined the Miss America contest up here.

CHICK.   Your father.... There's a case.

BRIAN.   Him too?

CHICK.   What're you crazy?

185

BRIAN.   You ever do anything with him?

CHICK.   *What?*

BRIAN.   I could handle it.

CHICK.   He's straight, ya little jerk. What is this? What you wanna see me for?

BRIAN.   What are you, Dracula? You got a beautiful face. I came to see my Uncle. Am I makin' you uncomfortable?

CHICK.   Yes. Very.

BRIAN.   Why?

CHICK.   What do you think? I'm embarrassed.

BRIAN.   I was thrilled, man, from the minute that Steve spit it out. He said you were hot.

CHICK.   Out. Out of here ...

BRIAN.   I'm only tryin' to act right.... Wait!

CHICK.   You think I'm some trick you can cruise now.?

BRIAN.   No no. I just was glad I had somebody for guidance.

CHICK.   You respect me.

BRIAN.   You're takin' it wrong.

CHICK.   There's disease out there. Death out there.

BRIAN.   I don't go with people, Chick.

CHICK.   "Uncle Chick."

BRIAN.   I'm being real with you. Have a little respect for me.

CHICK.   Geeeezus ... Brian.

BRIAN.   What?

CHICK.   You.

BRIAN.   So?

CHICK.   I'd rather you were straight.

BRIAN.   Why?

CHICK.   It's a hard life. It's hard.

BRIAN.   So you want me to cut my wrists?

CHICK.   You're young and it's just.... You outlive your little plans. You get small shots. You start over, twice, three times. It's a bitch.

BRIAN.   I seen the zoo out there, the skinheads, the cowboys and the teddy bears. I'm hip to the bullshit. It's the guys in loafers who go for me.

CHICK.   No lover?

BRIAN.   You think I'm gonna let some bar fly move in with

186

me?

CHICK. You need something ... somebody.

BRIAN. Not tonight. Tonight I got somebody.

CHICK. Don't ... even ... breathe it.

BRIAN. Wait ...

CHICK. C'mon punk. Out that door.

BRIAN. Steve told me what happened, so cut the malarkey.

CHICK. Steve knows shit.

BRIAN. His name was David Noonan. David Noonan. And he lived here with you and these are his boxes, right? And if we weren't queer there'd be a major funeral and Aunt Rosemary'd cry and you wouldn't be alone schlepping through his boxes at midnight in Greenwich Village for Godsake, wake up.

CHICK. I'm okay. I ... I think ...

BRIAN. You miss him. Don't you? So I thought I'd come ... see what you need ...

CHICK. I just need time.

BRIAN. You need more than time. I used to imitate your walk, you know that?

CHICK. I can't go into this.

BRIAN. Lemme stay over. Hang for a day.

CHICK. You crazy? We're related. We're Catholics.

BRIAN. I don't want to fuck you for Godsakes.

CHICK. *(Overlap.)* Shut up!

BRIAN. Catholics. We can't even go to Communion. They want us all to be priests or to get married. You're my Godfather. Tell me what I should do, where I should go.

CHICK. *(Ponders, hesitates.)* You're good. You're good. You hear?

BRIAN. Damn right and I love bein' Brian. I love this city. Gotham man. At night I look at the lit-up buildings. Empire State, man. I love the stink of the streets, the smoke, the colors. I love myself and I'm not chicken shit. I take care of Brian and I can take care of you, too.

CHICK. You a missionary or something?

BRIAN. When that architect told me tonight that you were like me, I swear I got on fire. There's like a mirror thing when I look at you. I see me. I have no confusion around you. We're like ... out of the same place.

CHICK. Brian ... Jesus.

BRIAN. I'll stay over, sleep with my clothes on. I'll clean up.... Sleep near ya, hold ya' hand.

CHICK. No good Brian.

BRIAN. *Hands* is all I'm sayin'. Please.

CHICK. You'll meet somebody.

BRIAN. Don't send me out there. It's all strangers out there. I'll make breakfast.

CHICK. Go. Please.

BRIAN. Cut it out Chick. Lemme hold ya. I'm all ya got and you're all I got. *(Chick folds his arms, remains frozen. Brian turns away.)* Oh, God ...

CHICK. Brian? *(Chick touches his shoulder. Brian turns quickly, surprises Chick and grabs him.)*

BRIAN. Don't worry. I'm here ... I'm here ...

END

HIS DISH

CHARACTERS

JAMES — a middle-class, middle-aged country man recently turned city man.

WILLIAM — a middle-class, middle-aged country man.

EDNA — a middle-class, middle-aged newlywed, big city nurse.

SETTING

A dining table in a rustic mountain home.

HIS DISH

A dining table. James and William sit opposite one another. Edna is in the middle. James sits sideways, his back is almost to the audience, so that when he moves away, his big dish and place setting are more downstage than any other prop. William has nothing before him, just the clean surface of the table on which there is a big set of car keys in conspicuous view. William reads a newspaper. Edna is so in love with James, her new husband, she just looks at him adoringly.

JAMES.   Now you see this breakfast here. This is the main reason I married Edna. Food. Now William while the fryin' pan's still hot, you be a fool not to let this sweet woman go in there and whip you up some eggs Benedict.

EDNA.   *(Hurt.)* Leave your brother be Jimmie. He ain't hungry, obviously.

JAMES.   How'd I do without this angel woman all them years?

WILLIAM.   Beats me.

EDNA.   When William changes his mind I'll race into that kitchen and cook him a king's breakfast in the snap of his finger. He'll get hungry soon. Won't ya, William?

WILLIAM.   I'da made eggs for myself if I wanted eggs.

JAMES.   Well now, I gotta nature call so 'scuse me, but not till I get my candy kiss. *(He bends to Edna. She pecks at him.)* Gimme a chocolate covered raspberry jelly bar. *(They giggle, chuckle, coo, and kiss again.)* Mmmm ... make that jelly a little deeper. *(Kiss.)* Put some vanilla ice cream on top of that. *(Kiss.)* Now let me lick up them rainbow sprinkles. Ummmm. Now you take the cellophane off that box of French chocolates and I'll be back to taste 'em soon as I'm done washin' up my honey-face.

EDNA. Bye, Sweetie.

JAMES. Not for long.

EDNA. A minute'll seem forever. *(He exits. To William.)* God, I envy you ... *(He doesn't look up from his paper.)* ... havin' his blood in your veins.

WILLIAM. Don't be disgusting.

EDNA. Why don't you take advantage of our visit and let me baby you? He brought me up here just to have you meet me.

WILLIAM. How long you married to my brother?

EDNA. Two weeks.

WILLIAM. If I were you I'd grab those car keys and get the hell out of here before he gets back. You don't have a clue what you're into, Edna.

EDNA. Don't just drop that on me. What am I into?

WILLIAM. My brother's got what they call an imperial complex. The only kind of woman can stay married to that is a submissive, masochistic fool who enjoys being his ass-kissin' slave and servant — just like you were this morning.

EDNA. Now wait a minute. James told me your mother used to make sausages, eggs, and griddle cakes with ... with maple syrup ... so I ...

WILLIAM. Isn't that what you just made him?

EDNA. Yes, why not?

WILLIAM. How does it feel to be his mommy?

EDNA. Now wait a minute. A generous act is not ...

WILLIAM. Does the man ever get a meal for you?

EDNA. The poor guy can't cook.

WILLIAM. You do the laundry? You shop? You dust? Mop? Make the bed?

EDNA. I want to.

WILLIAM. You're a nurse, right? You put in how many hours?

EDNA. Eight, sometimes ten. Sometimes twelve.

WILLIAM. More than him?

EDNA. Not necessarily.

WILLIAM. Does he wash out your panties at night?

EDNA.   You're awful.

WILLIAM.   Does he take the garbage out? What does he do?

EDNA.   So we assume traditional roles ...

WILLIAM.   He won't do a shit-ball thing. I remember the king of the mountain when he was the little *prince,* okay? And as far as eggs and sausage are concerned, my mother was makin' them before all this cholesterol taboo was out there, okay? As a nurse you should know better than to put that poison in fronta him. There's nitrites in the sausages, garbage fat in the eggs, garbage sugar in the syrup.

EDNA.   You think you're gonna live forever?

WILLIAM.   Some of us is gonna die sooner than others.

EDNA.   So what if I "poach" you a couple of farm fresh egg whites? That's the advantage you have living here in the country. Freshness. You don't have our smog.

WILLIAM.   I don't have your tension.

EDNA.   Right.

WILLIAM.   I don't have your murder.

EDNA.   Okay.

WILLIAM.   Your incest.

EDNA.   You probably get more of that up here.

WILLIAM.   We don't need incest, Edna. We don't even need wives. We have sheep up here.

EDNA.   I think we're politically incompatible.

WILLIAM.   Lockin' horns you mean.

EDNA.   Exactly.

WILLIAM.   See ya again sometime.

EDNA.   *(Beat.)* Is that a grape arbor I see down the hill? *(Beat.)* William, for God's sake. You didn't make our wedding. He wanted you for his best man. My God.

WILLIAM.   Ain't that tough ditty?

EDNA.   So, poor sucker that he is, he ... gets me and his dogs, drags us up here, for what? For you to meet me.

WILLIAM.   Dogs shit on my rug.

EDNA.   They're puppies.

WILLIAM.   Who cleaned it up? Right. Take a look at the end of the table. Look.

EDNA.   I'm looking.

WILLIAM. What do you see there, Edna?

EDNA. A half-empty glass of orange juice.

WILLIAM. Open your eyes.

EDNA. His dirty dish. A napkin ...

WILLIAM. His dirty dish.

EDNA. His dirty dish.

WILLIAM. Who's gonna take that away? Wanna make a bet? When his slave died, my poor mother, James musta figured, 'gotta find me a woman who will kiss my ass just like Mama did, a pretty woman with nice puckered up lips like yours ...

EDNA. That's a horrible thing to say to me.

WILLIAM. Horrible thing is his dish. Just *look* at that dirty dish. Waitin' for you to bring it to the kitchen, for you to wash, to dry and put away, just like it was for you to cook his damned eggs, his damn bacon and toast, and serve it all up to your master. Well, what're you waitin' for? Ain't you gonna pick up that dish like a good little ass kisser? *(Edna looks away, as if to suppress emotion.)* You shoulda gotten to know the man better, Edna.

EDNA. He's not a criminal for God's sake.

WILLIAM. Maybe you know more about him than I do.

EDNA. It doesn't have to be fifty-fifty.

WILLIAM. It doesn't have to be ninety-ten either. Or a hundred-zero like it is with you.

EDNA. Oh God help me. Shit. *(James enters.)*

JAMES. What's the matter here?

EDNA. Nothing. We ...

JAMES. You look like you both just got some bad news here.

EDNA. We were talking about when you were both small.

JAMES. What you tell her William?

WILLIAM. Just memories.

JAMES. That's what I brought her here for. This is your new family. *(Edna stands.)* No. Here. I'll clear this stuff away. *(He lifts the dish. She grabs it.)*

EDNA. I'll do it.

JAMES. No.

EDNA. Let me go. I'm taking this plate inside, James, and I'm ... *(James wins the tug o' war with the dish, pushing Edna back*

194

onto her chair.)
JAMES. Dang it, Edna. You're gonna do as I say and sit. Jesus, what come over you? *(She stares.)* Now sit the hell back. Sit back! *(She sits back.)* Lemme see them lips pucker. Puckerrrr. Them. You're gonna laugh. *(She, laughs, nervously and with shame.)* Now I want a slew of kisses. *(One kiss.)* No. I want a big Black forest cherry chocolate with whip cream on top kinda kiss. *(Kiss.)* Now. Lemme have a mocha maple sugar cream with a cherry on top. *(Kiss.)* Where was the cherry? Gimme the cherry. *(Kiss.)* Now let's have a ... Marzipan walnut chocolate covered tangerine kiss. *(Kiss.)* Mnnnnn. My favorite. So you and William got to know one another, did ya?
EDNA. Yes.
JAMES. What he tell ya?
EDNA. Huh? Nothing. *(Still holding his dish, he bends and kisses his wife.)*
JAMES.   Oh yeah? Show him who you belong to. I want a giant pineapple-mocha mousse kiss, with a praline coating and a warm caramel heart *(Kiss.)* Mnnnn. *(Kiss.)*
EDNA. James, I can't ...
JAMES. Show him your double baked Alaska, hot hot fudge sundae whip cream banana split cherry syrup ...
EDNA. Stop. I gotta get outta here.
JAMES. Not till I get my double baked Alaska, hot ...
EDNA. *(She jumps up, wipes her mouth.)* You're disgusting. I hate you. The both of you.
JAMES. What? *(William puts his paper up before his face. Edna grabs the car keys and runs.)* No. Don't you do this to me ... Ednaaaah? *(He turns to William.)* What did you tell her? *(Lights fade.)*

END

BUTTERBALL

CHARACTERS

HANDSOME HUGH
TOM
BUTTERBALL
MOTHER (Gladys)
MILDRED

SETTING

A long table set for a feast, decorated with dark blue, white and blood red bunting. Back stage a large artichoke and a fresh-killed roasted human wait to be carried on. All characters wear large yellow turkey feet.

BUTTERBALL

Handsome Hugh and Tom come out, set the table and disappear. An early American hymn plays as Butterball, Gladys and Mildred come on. Gladys wheels a table full of props for dinner while Butterball, holding a crystal dish of black olives comes to the curtain to talk to the audience. Despite their turkey feet, the women wear 1950s prom dresses. As Butterball speaks, she spits olive out pits out onto the stage.

BUTTERBALL.   Aunt Mildred lost her humanity in Chile, you know? South America? In the Peace Corps. She got raped by a military buzzard named Pinochet. Don't worry. She pecked holes in her eggs for a year not to be mother to a machismo dictator's child. That's what made a turkey out of her. My eggs will remain unfertile till I'm married, unless I meet an ostrich. They turn me on. Anyway they had a perfectly fine democratic government down there and President Allende somehow insulted some corporate giant like ITT and they got Nixon, our then president, to use our tax money to set up the very generalissimo who made a turkey out of Aunt Mildred. Better to be a living turkey than a dead human. I'm sure you have your story too. My name is.... Guess.

GLADYS.   Butterballll! Stop gobbling up the olives.

MILDRED.   Gladys, are you crazy setting the table with banners? We can't celebrate losing our humanity!

GLADYS.   We saved our lives. Mildred. Now don't spoil the holiday.

MILDRED.   We just been made turkeys of is all.

GLADYS.   You pay mind to Butterball and be thankful, Mildred. Handsome Hugh is here. He waited so patiently for you to come home.

MILDRED.   Oh please, no, I'll die if he's been turned into a turkey too.

GLADYS.   There's only a few humans left, dear. For breeding. That big mouth of yours is gonna make trouble.

MILDRED.   I shouldn't've come to this awful party.

GLADYS.   Celebrate your survival.

MILDRED.   You call being turned into a turkey, survival?

GLADYS.   Thank the Lord you exist in any form whatsoever.

BUTTERBALL.   She just loves being an old maid, Mother. Leave her be.

MILDRED.   When are you gonna get this kid into therapy.

GLADYS.   She's a normal teenager going through her pecking stage.

MILDRED.   Pecking, my ass. She's a class-A bitch.

GLADYS.   Butterball you go check on the human now. *(Butterball starts to leave.)* And it needs to cool off so don't pick at it. Millie when I walk into a house and smell that odor of a human roasting I get a cozy feeling in my breast. I say, let the winter come.

MILDRED.   I want to restore my humanhood, Gladys. It can be done.

GLADYS.   Shut up. It's dangerous to talk that way.

MILDRED.   Look at us! It's all turned around. We're cannibals eating humans.

GLADYS.   You give thanks.

MILDRED.   They're carcinogenic. There's lead in their water. They're full of X-rays, anti-biotics, they're not freshly killed and they are us.

GLADYS.   You're not gonna make a human out of me. I saw ours killed. I picked it out myself.

MILDRED.   Some come from morgues.

GLADYS.   Oh where'd you hear that?

MILDRED.   National Poultry Radio.

GLADYS.   You will spoil anything of mine. Butterball go get your father. Oh, *(Enter Tom.)* there you are. You took forever in the shower, Sweetheart.

TOM.   I was just standing there for some reason.

GLADYS.   Getting water in your sinuses.

TOM.   Yeah.

GLADYS.   Didn't you wear your nose cap?

TOM.   I didn't think of it.

BUTTERBALL.   The roasted man has an asshole, Daddy.

GLADYS.   Eeeek!   MILDRED.   Poooo!

TOM.   Ain't she bright?

MILDRED.   She's disgusting. How would she even know it's a male?

BUTTERBALL.   You know that paper package with the heart and liver and all that they stuff up him after he's killed?

TOM.   Listen to this.

MILDRED.   Stop her!

BUTTERBALL.   Well there was his watchermacallit.

MILDRED.   God, get me out of here.

BUTTERBALL.   I saw it.

GLADYS.   Butterball, tell Uncle Hugh to bring in the human and I'll get the.... *(Butterball and Gladys exit momentarily.)* Come with me.

MILDRED.   Where's my coat? Tom. Help me out of this hell, Tom. We are not turkeys, for God's sake. I can't eat a human being.

TOM.   They cooked you an artichoke.

MILDRED.   Where in the good Bejesus-hell is my bag? Oh screw it. *(Leaving, she bumps into the roasted human being wheeled in by Handsome Hugh and Gladys. On top of the roasted human is a gigantic artichoke. Butterball follows triumphantly.)*

GLADYS.   Millie, you know Handsome Hugh. *(Suddenly, it gets serious and realistic as the two recall better times and their deep love.)*

HANDSOME HUGH.   Millie ... God, you look beautiful.

MILDRED.   No, Hugh, I ...

HANDSOME HUGH.   I missed you so much, Millie.

MILDRED.   Oh, God, Hugh. How could you let them do this to you?

HANDSOME HUGH.   I changed political parties and suddenly I turned around and I was like this.

BUTTERBALL.   I want a foot. I want both feet.

GLADYS.   You wait with the rest of us. Why Mildred, you're crying!

MILDRED.   They're so elegant and large and powerful. How could we have done this to them?

GLADYS.   Grow up. Butterball, come away.

MILDRED.   Hugh admits he's not thrilled to be a turkey anymore.

HANDSOME HUGH.   At least we're the cooks and they're the food.

MILDRED.   No. No ...

HANDSOME HUGH.   If we didn't create a market for them, they'd be extinct. There'd just be a few street bums left out there.

GLADYS.   Oh, sit and eat your artichoke. You're with your family. *(Exhaustedly, Mildred plops in her chair before her artichoke.)*

BUTTERBALL.   You think it's so chic to be a vegetarian. Well artichokes scream when they get picked and they moan all the way home from the store and Ugggh. *(Cough, cough.)* ... the pepper ... when you put it in them, it chokes them and the garlic, it chokes them too and the salt, Owwww, it burns their inside. But when you pour olive oil on them and turn on the flame.... Agggggggg. Agggggggg! They sweat, they burn ... but do they die? Oh no. Not even when you rip off their leaves. Uhg ... and run your teeth down the inside. Ummm, throwing the skin away as if it were garbage. No, but when you bite into their heart ... they try to prick you with their little prickers, they stick pins in your tongue with their last ounce of strength but does that stop people like you? No. You go on chompin' on it's heart till you swallow it and does it die then? No. The heart goes on inside you till it turns to shit!

MILDRED.   Go stand in the rain.

GLADYS.   Uncle Hugh. Say grace.

MILDRED.   Say grace and I'm gonna do something quite rash.

TOM.   Okay, now touch wings. Hit it Hugh.

HANDSOME HUGH.   I.... You Tom. It's your house.

TOM.   Oh Lord, we thank Thee, for helping us to be good turkeys and for giving us dominion over this planet and all living things and for providing us with this lovely food which we are about to eat.

MILDRED.   You just murdered this man and are about to eat him. This is like a big disgusting myth being enacted here.

GLADYS.   Amen.

MILDRED. Aaaaamen? Gladys you lemming, is that all you know how to say?

HANDSOME HUGH. Let the old bird finish his prayer.

TOM. Yes, the Lord'd given us wings to remind us that our destiny is up there ... *(All look.)* Among the.... Among the ...

BUTTERBALL. There's a bunch of stage lights up there.

GLADYS. Shut-up, Butterball. Amen and that's final.

BUTTERBALL. The foot. The foot. I want the foot! *(Overlap some of the following.)*

GLADYS. Give her some cider.

TOM. Pass me that cider there.

BUTTERBALL. I want a foot I said, I want both feet.

GLADYS. Oh give her a foot and shut her up. Watch those toe bones. Land sakes there's enough here to feed fifty of us. *(Gladys is serving the meat.)*

TOM. We'll have sandwiches tomorrow.

BUTTERBALL. On pumpernickel with mayonnaise!

HANDSOME HUGH. Salt and pepper.

TOM. What part for you Hugh?

HANDSOME HUGH. None for me.

TOM. You'll have some if Millie has some. C'mon Millie.

BUTTERBALL. *("You say potato, I say potahto.")* I love the fingers. I love the toes. I love the liver and the Pope's nose. The liver, the wee wee, the dark meat, the pee-pee. Let's all eat until we fall. *(Some take up Butterball's chant and repeat. Hugh holds his ears. Mildred pulls a revolver from her bag, in terror.)*

TOM. Grab a slice of human everybody.

GLADYS. Now toast. Toast. *(All but Hugh and Mildred hold up a human part and a fancy champagne glass.)*

TOM. To Richard Nixon. Hugh. Won't do you no good to side with Millie. The authorities are comin' for her. I took care of that.

GLADYS. That wasn't necessary. *(Handsome Hugh sheepishly holds up a drum stick.)*

TOM / ALL BUT MILDRED. Yaaaaayyy!

GLADYS. To President Johnson and Vietnam. C'mon Millie.

HANDSOME HUGH. To Somalia and ...

GLADYS. To the marriage of Millie and Hugh.

203

MILDRED. No. Never. I will never ...

BUTTERBALL. Hey Aunt Millie, Look what I found in the garbage! *(Butterball pulls a human head out of a shopping bag. Mildred screams, runs to the curtain and fires into the air. The turkeys — Tom, Gladys and Butterball — gobble-gobble hysterically and scatter for protection. In the sudden silence, Mildred stands, terribly shaken. In a sort of trance she bows respectfully to the roasted human.)*

MILDRED. Will you excuse me? I have to go home. *(Nearly tripping over the head, she looks down at it.)* Excuse me. *(Addressing the head, then the audience.)* Any of you turkeys remember ... before? *(She walks into the house with her smoking gun, in a state of total disintegration, appealing to the audience.)* Do you know where I used to live? Take me home? Anybody. Remember Deepak Chopra? Gail? Jonathan? You there? Anybody? Linda? Linda, you still hiding somewhere? Debbie, did they get you too? Carol? How about Bobby Newfeld? Anybody? Christopher? Remember me? Diane? Richie? Jessica? Anybody here know me?

HOUSE MADE OF AIR

CHARACTER

MATILDE

On September 11, 1963, the Presidential Palace in Santiago, Chile, was bombed by the Army of General Augusto Pinochet. With help from President Nixon and Mr. Kissinger, Chile's economy was nearly squeezed to death. The CIA paid strikers to quit working. Sabotage and subterfuge were employed to bring down President Allende, a democratically elected president, and to replace him with Pinochet, a renowned dictator. Allende was killed in the bombing. The Fulbright Commission and The Frank Church Committee hearings on covert operations abroad, proved the participation of Kissinger, Nixon and the CIA. With the help of the United States government, General Pinochet headed one of the most shockingly violent and dictatorial regimes in the history of modern politics that lasted over eighteen years. The film, *Missing* with Jack Lemmon, exposed the nightmare. Isabella Allende, daughter of the assassinated president wrote, *House of the Spirits,* a novel about the incident, which became a film with Meryl Streep and Jeremy Irons. The violence of Pinochet and the Chilean army toward its own people remains an enigma of human nature that mystifies psychologists and historians to this day.

Pablo Neruda, the Chilean poet and winner of the Nobel Prize for literature was a supporter of the democratically elected Salvador Allende and was himself, for a time, a senator in that government. Neruda, a powerful voice in Chile, was on Pinochet's hit list even as the poet was dying of prostate cancer at his summer home in Valparaiso. War ships had gathered outside his windows. Busloads of soldiers surrounded his house and stood in every window. Matilde, Neruda's wife, ordered an ambulance and they attempted to escape to Bella Vista, to their city home in Santiago. But Pinochet's men stopped them frequently at junta road blocks, deliberately harassing the dying man and hastening his death.

HOUSE MADE OF AIR

A dark room in their house in Isla Negra, a summer resort near Valparaiso, Chile, overlooking the sea. Matilde has just returned from Paris, exiled from Chile since 1974. She's dressed in mourning for the occasion, in a summery black dress and a hat with a veil. Things have not been touched in all those years since she and Pablo left the house together. Matilde brushes aside dusty curtains and enters the dark shut off dancing room which contains nothing but an old stand-up Victrola and a table upon which are piles of old 78 RPM record albums, many loose 78s, two cordial glasses and a decanter of liquor that has dried up. She blows dust out of one of the glasses, wets a finger and rims the glass to taste the past. She opens the cover of the Victrola, lifts the needle arm, puts it down on a tango record, then quickly closes the cover. The song plays mutely under her speaking and drearily winds out before long.

MATILDE. Four busloads of soldiers surrounded this house, our summer house. They overturned his bed and tore up the mattress with their bayonets. I brought him in here, off the dining room where we used to dance. "When the ambulance comes, I will not ride on my back," he said. "But of course, you will sit up, Darling. You may sit up" ... but I was sure they would kill us before the ambulance arrived. Then, the loud siren screaming must have intimidated the Captain and some of them even helped us into the ambulance. He just fell back on the pillow too weak to sit up and he turned his face from me. I touched his arm. "The world is watching." I said. "But I am dying." He whispered. "And still," I said, "you are the greatest voice in your land and the greatest poet in the world."

"For me this Victrola was the hardest thing to leave behind, and our music. *(She starts re-winding it.)* Our memories spoke through this, our songs, his operas, the tangos, the meringues and American fox trots. He would wear white at dinner and make my coffee and bring it here and he would grab me here and dance with me even when he didn't feel well. One morning a friend called from Washington and told him that Nixon was going to get rid of Allende. There were tapes of Nixon saying: "I want to hear Chile's economy ... scream." This put him in bed. "An American president replacing a democracy with a dictatorship? Why? Because Allende was giving milk to the poor, power to the poor, land to the poor and the multi-national corporations were losing their slaves." He paced all night. "Chile is dying and I am dying with it." "Pablo," I said. "Politics have always been this way." But he kept pacing and muttering "Nixon, Nixon, Nixon." Sweden telephoned offering asylum. Mexico would send a plane that night but he wanted to die at our house in Santiago, with his books, his poets and musicians so ... we left all this music behind.

At every junta roadblock, soldiers flung open the ambulance doors and dragged him out. "Who are you?" He asked. They were not the police. The police would have recognized him. So politely I spoke to the leader. "This man is a friend of President Allende." I smiled. He threw me to the ground. "Allende was executed this morning." He said. These were our own people. That's what made it so hard for him. They scattered his pain-killers in the sewers, accused us of drug possession. They threw him into the weeds at the roadside and let him lie in the sun. "Shoot him," I screamed, "shoot him, you bastards and then tell the general what you did." But it was the general who gave them their orders. He didn't want my poet to enter his city in triumph. The general wanted that for himself, to kill the light, to make the poet's country dark. So when the light comes on again, the general will be the light. And so the poet who was gifted with Nobel's prize, received the dictator's kiss of death on a dirt road. Tortures, war, murder, burnings, rapes, filled the next two decades. And that is how the devil became the light.

I laid him out in our house but they had been there first ... to burn his books. They broke the pipes on the second floor and the stairs were a waterfall.... Papers ... with his handwriting ... floated around his body. People walked up to him in galoshes, in bare feet, wading, through water and paper and books. Poems floated around him like little ships. The soldiers took names of all our friends, but they came anyway, knowing it could kill them too. Poets singing, musicians playing. Guitars. Love came. It fell to its knees in the water. It showed it's breast to the guns. It wrapped it's lips around their canons and when the trigger was pulled, love broke apart like a rose. I burned the petals. I swallowed the ashes and ... left ... for France. *(She puts on a tango record and puts the cover down so the music plays mutely under.)*

When I hear his music I picture Pablo. When I say his name, I smell his body. When I read his poems I taste his lips. I speak his words and I feel the vibrations of his voice in my lungs. His poems lift my body and carry me up a staircase made of air. I smell the sea and the valleys through his windows, I see his horses running wild. My curtains hang like banners from his stars. Every morning he takes me to the upper floors to make love and when night comes we fall, softly, like people in parachutes, down to the ballroom floor. The breeze though the keyholes becomes our music. The thunder is our walls. Confetti falls like rain into our rooms. We are dancing in his rain. We are dancing long after the moon appears. We dance from house to house, from ballroom to ballroom, we dance till dawn in all his houses made of air. Pablo ... *(Pablo has come out, a man, dressed in a white suit. He lifts the cover of the Victrola. The music is loud and rich. He takes her rapturously into his arms and dances with her until a sudden blackout.)*

END

FUR HAT

CHARACTERS

JANETTE
DON

FUR HAT

Janette is over fifty. She is beautiful and expensively dressed, including her fur hat.

Don is also over fifty. He teaches in the building, so he wears a cardigan sweater, shirt and tie.

Janette and Don were once married to each other. They haven't seen one another in many years. Wearing a beautiful fur hat, Janette sits alone at a table for four in a university cafeteria, eating as she works on a speech that she is to deliver in an hour or so. She has expressed full territoriality over the table. Her coat and books, not one, but two cameras, scarf and sweater, bag, briefcase, pocketbook, and notebooks occupy table and spare chair. She uses reading glasses which she removes whenever she looks away from reading matter, for her eyes are perfect otherwise. She fills a glass with milk from a small container, then tastes it with uncertainty. She eats a Danish pastry hungrily.

Don enters, carrying a tray with a coffee and a Danish. He wears a shirt and tie with no jacket, as if his coat and other possessions are somewhere else in the building. He works there. Janette is only visiting. A notebook and pen are pressed under his arm. The cafeteria is supposedly crowded, though our set reveals only the one table and its four chairs.

We are aware from the frustration in Don's search that Janette's table is Don's only bet. He sits at the empty chair as she, with glasses still on, removes things from here and there in order to make the sharing democratic.

Both work as they eat, glancing indifferently at one another until Janette takes off the fur hat. Soon after, they recognize one another, and Janette attempts a getaway, slowly gather-

213

ing her things, but Don decides not to let her off the hook. He speaks before she can stand up.

DON.   My God. Is it you?

JAN.   I don't think I've changed as much as you have.

DON.   You're not teaching here are you?

JAN.   I've been invited to lecture. You teach here, obviously.

DON.   Just one course. I teach ... *(Embarrassed.)*

JAN.   What?

DON.   Industrial geography.

JAN.   Still obsessed with money?

DON.   I'm just teaching about it, not making much of it.

JAN.   You made your mother happy. You're a teacher in a university. Now if money was sex with students, you'd be a millionaire.

DON.   I get to take my students on the Circle Line boat around Manhattan. Did you ever take that tour?

JAN.   Ugh ...

DON.   It's fun.

JAN.   Someday one of those boats is going to sink.

DON.   The Statue of Liberty wouldn't allow it.

JAN.   Even iron women bend over for you?

DON.   You weren't iron.

JAN.   Don't I know it.

DON.   The women in my life were anything but iron.

JAN.   How did they stand up after you were through with them?

DON.   You kept this anger fresh and ready for twenty years?

JAN.   Forty years.

DON.   The first twenty were all right.

JAN.   The first nineteen. The year you walked out was no fun.

DON.   So give me nineteen.

JAN.   I'll give you nothing. *(She smells the milk.)* Since you sat down I don't trust this milk. It seems to have gone sour.

DON.   Always sarcastic.

JAN.   Smell it. *(He does.)*

DON.   Always right. Shall I get you a fresh one?

JAN.   No, thanks. I've got to go.

DON. You look prosperous.

JAN. *(She laughs at his unconscious reference to money.)* I sell a picture now and then.

DON. I've seen them. Expensive camera. Expensive hat. Must keep your head warm.

JAN. I bought it in Russia last week.

DON. Must be making money.

JAN. Always money.

DON. Always the martyr.

JAN. Go fuck a schizophrenic student or something.

DON. Bitter.

JAN. Experienced.

DON. I'm older now.

JAN. Your eyes are still sex hungry.

DON. You misread them. I'm proud of your work.

JAN. Because of the money part?

DON. Because of your articles. What's going on in Russia. That's very important.

JAN. You think the Russians admire the United States?

DON. I don't want to talk politics.

JAN. You think your government knows what we have done to them?

DON. I couldn't care less.

JAN. You should have married Lina Wertmueller. She'd have burned your capitalist cock off.

DON. You a neo-communist now?

JAN. No, I'm a distributist, each person has a right to land.

DON. Still against abortion?

JAN. Of course.

DON. Still got your shoelaces tied together, and you wonder why you can't walk.

JAN. I walked here. I made it all the way through Poland, Yugoslavia, Italy, Haiti. I told off the Pope. I photographed Auschwitz. I told off the Prime Minister of Israel. I spent four hours at the Havana airport drinking gin and tonics with you know who, I spent two weeks in France with Marquez because he wouldn't come to the United States now even if they let him. I made some of your precious money. And in Russia I bought myself a fur hat.

DON.   You sound like a man boasting.

JAN.   I learned from a pompous husband.

DON.   Who gave you his tongue in bed a thousand nights.

JAN.   I'm not a robot. I was born to love and I tried.

DON.   Your hands are shaking. Why are you shaking? Janette?

JAN.   Your corpse is kicking inside of me.

DON.   You're not dead inside of me.

JAN.   You never felt a kick from inside. You're a man. All sealed up neatly with just a tiny hole in your long prick. I would like you to get pregnant, in your balls. I'd like the baby to tear you open and explode out of you. I'd like you to moan and have a hundred Kotexes stuffed inside your bleeding hole, each one contributed by one of the students you made love to. *(Pause.)*

DON.   I'm glad you finally got it off your chest. What lecture are you giving today?

JAN.   A Danforth Lecture on Russian poverty.

DON.   So poverty is paying off.

JAN.   I care about them. They're acquainted with their dignity. Not like Americans who steal the land then call it free. Not like whores like you who believe that profit makes personhood.

DON.   It pays the rent.

JAN.   We pay the rent for a world that already belongs to us. The Russians don't idealize democracy. They have to fight for a goddamn banana. That's their freedom …

DON.   I find that a trifle hysterical.

JAN.   … and they're ready to die on the cross for it.

DON.   Did you become a Catholic now?

JAN.   Go to hell. Keep teaching profit. Especially to young women. It'll keep your cock hard.

DON.   Speaking of kids, I heard from Lily. She's pregnant.

JAN.   You found something out. Do you know your grandson had an ear operation?

DON.   Which one?

JAN.   Richard's son.

DON.   I … should visit Richard.

JAN.   Not Thursdays. I'll be there. Now, if you'll excuse me

I have to throw up before my lecture. *(She stands.)*
DON. Janette ...
JAN. Yes.
DON. It was nice being at a table together. It reminded me of ...
JAN. Go teach profit. *(He stands and comes to her.)*
DON. Kiss me goodbye. *(She finds this funny.)*
JAN. Mr. Push Button. What if I didn't bump into you here? Would you have taken the trouble to look me up?
DON. No. A friendly kiss.
JAN. Go kiss that last woman you kissed.
DON. I love you.
JAN. Of course. And I love you.
DON. So?
JAN. So it snowed in the Bahamas last year.
DON. You still won't show your feelings.
JAN. Maybe not, but I learned to have them. That I've learned. Look at you. Standing there you remind me of so much waste. My hands shake. You know why? They want to touch your face at the same time they want to slap it. Your tired eyes make me want to cry. Am I having feelings?
DON. Yes.
JAN. But so what? Right? Are you still happily married to your student? What is she, forty now? Forty-two?
DON. Okay. Goodbye Janette.
JAN. See you in Heaven. *(She prepares to leave, then starts to do so, leaving her fur hat behind.)*
DON. Janette! *(She turns.)* Your hat! *(She returns to him, takes it, but he doesn't let it go.)* You allowed an animal to die for a hat?
JAN. It's fake for all I know.
DON. She still lies to herself. Just the way you lie to yourself about pollution, about overpopulation.
JAN. You people are gassing the world, you're just automatons who don't understand life so you destroy it.
DON. You still believe in God?
JAN. Only to spite you.
DON. And how much land are you going to distribute to each person two hundred years from now?

JAN.   Let the whole plan blow up in our faces. Let God take care of it. Give me my hat.

DON.   No.

JAN.   Okay. Keep it. *(She takes the milk from her tray and throws it in his face. He laughs genuinely.)* Masochist.

DON.   This fur is real. You killed a living thing.

JAN.   Shut up. I never gave it a second thought.

DON.   You're violent and you refuse to admit it.

JAN.   *(About to weep.)* And what are you? What blood did you cause to spill? What pain? Who left you when the first wrinkle appeared? Who left you when the kids went to college? For a student as old as your daughter? You tore the skin off my back and made a hat out of me.

DON.   Keep it.

JAN.   Give the thing to some poor cold person. *(She turns. He throws the hat after her with enormous hurt and anger.)*

DON.   You give it back to the animal whose back you tore it off. *(She picks up the hat and throws it in his face.)*

JAN.   Give me back what you tore away from me. Wipe up my blood, wipe away the long winters alone, the embarrassment, the horror.

DON.   How can I? *(She takes a cloth handkerchief from her bag.)* We make mistakes ...

JAN.   How can I give that poor thing back to its owner?

DON.   If I knew I would tell you. *(His eyes beg for forgiveness.)*

JAN.   You stupid ... stupid man ... *(He stoops, picks up the hat, and holds it out to her. She takes it, with fear, with guilt.)* What ... kind of animal is this made of? Do you know?

DON.   A fox, a rabbit? I dunno.

JAN.   Poor thing. Here, wipe your face. *(Her white handkerchief. He wipes his face, offers it back.)* Throw it away. It'll make your wife jealous if she finds it in your pocket.

DON.   I'll keep it if you don't mind.

JAN.   Hold it. *(She takes a flash photo of him.)* Thanks. Goodbye.

END

BUS STOP DINER

CHARACTERS

MARTIN
REYNOLDS
WAITER

BUS STOP DINER

Martin is sitting in a booth at a breakfast diner reading the New York Times. *Reynolds is on his way there, passing out flyers.*

WAITER.   Are you ready to order breakfast, Sir?

MARTIN.   After eight cups of your coffee I am so wired I'm seeing spots right there. See them?

WAITER.   Oh Jesus. I'll get you some de-caf.

MARTIN.   No more coffee.

WAITER.   Then you're ready to order. *(Hands him a menu.)*

MARTIN.   I could never eat now.

WAITER.   Bad news in the Arts and Leisure section?

MARTIN.   What?

WAITER.   You're the playwright. Whatzizname. Right?

MARTIN.   That's me. Whatzizname.

WAITER.   You know I can't allow you to hog the New York *Times.* It's for all my customers.

MARTIN.   I've only had it a few minutes here.

WAITER.   You've been tearing it to pieces for the past two hours. You gotta buy your own if you wanna make love to it. Now gimme ... *(Gets into a tug over the paper, Martin wins.)*

MARTIN.   Who the hell do you think you are?

WAITER.   I'm James your waiter. You started reading at eight. Now it's ten. Believe me, the shorter the better. Think David Mamet.

MARTIN.   Take it.

WAITER.   Thank you.

MARTIN.   And there was no bad news in it, about me or David.

WAITER.   They'll nail you. They nailed him. They fried me.

MARTIN.   You're a playwright?

WAITER.   Was. Was. *(James departs. Martin takes out a portable telephone and dials.)*

MARTIN.   William Morris? Gilbert Parker please. Gilbert?

Don't come tonight. The director's a wacko. Never. I never *met* the guy till last night and he invited the freakin' critics no less. What theatre? It's a church with an organ the size of a Brontosaurus and someone who can't play, plays throughout my play. No you don't know any of the actors. Their main credit is they were all turned down by Uta Hagen. *(Unseen, Reynolds enters carrying note pads, props, rolled up posters and flyers.)* Give him notes how? I was supposed to at nine but he hasn't dared show his face ...

REYNOLDS. Good morning.

MARTIN. Oh Jesus. He's standing over me. Yeah. Lemme go ...

REYNOLDS. I left two messages on your machine.

MARTIN. A crock, Reynolds. You said The Bus Stop Diner at nine. I'm here since eight and now it's ten according to the ... ex-playwright over there.

REYNOLDS. No. I said I'd call you first and I called, I called *at nine.*

MARTIN. My bus leaves in fifteen minutes. Forget the notes. Forget my play. Close it.

REYNOLDS. Close it?

MARTIN. Close it.

REYNOLDS. Tonight's your opening. We need you.

MARTIN. My wife is choking upstate in some emergency room. She can't breathe.... She can't talk ...

REYNOLDS. I know the show was off last night but that's good luck.

MARTIN. The organ Reynolds. An organ in my play can never be good luck.

REYNOLDS. *(Writes.)* Get ... organ ... tuned.

MARTIN. *It's too late to tune the organ.*

REYNOLDS. Oh.

MARTIN. I don't *want* an organ. An organ has nothing whatever to do with my play.

REYNOLDS. See, I didn't hear it. I was backstage.

MARTIN. Imagine the Titanic sucking up the Atlantic and choking on the ice cubes?

MARTIN and REYNOLDS. ... *that was the organ.*

REYNOLDS. Got it. *(Writes.)* Cut ... organ.... I wanted to ask about my blocking.

MARTIN. What blocking? I thought that was Tai Chi.

REYNOLDS. Ha. See, the actors knew you were out there.

MARTIN. Close my play.

REYNOLDS. You have no faith in your work?

MARTIN. My work? My work?

REYNOLDS. Okay – okay – my work. Gimme the highlights.

MARTIN. How optimistic of you!

REYNOLDS. Well what was the worst thing?

MARTIN. You have no set.

REYNOLDS. I ... I wanted no set.

MARTIN. Why no set?

REYNOLDS. Purity.

MARTIN. Purity needs to be designed.

REYNOLDS. *(Writes.)* Purity needs ...

MARTIN. *Stop writing!*

REYNOLDS. I'm taking down your adjustments.

MARTIN. Do you know the Dalai Lama?

REYNOLDS. Uh.... Not personally.

MARTIN. It doesn't matter 'cause the Dalai, the Pope and Billy Graham combined could not adjust what you've done to my play. If you don't close it yourself, the critics will close it for you.

REYNOLDS. Oh no. Just can't.... That can never happen. I paid for eighty performances. In advance. Can't happen.

MARTIN. *(Overlap.)* You paid for eighty...?

REYNOLDS. Two months theatre rental. Salaries. Advertising. All paid up.

MARTIN. If your investors invite you on a ride, say to the docks tomorrow night? And you smell a bucket of cement in the car...?

REYNOLDS. You're unhappy with my direction.

MARTIN. I ... am unhappy with Elia Kazan and Jose Quintero. How could I be happy with you? I counted on this production to pay my mortgage and I am headed out of town as fast as my legs could carry me so what does that say to you, Reynolds?

REYNOLDS. I am not doing your play to make you happy ...
MARTIN. The dawn is here.
REYNOLDS. ... or to please the critics or any damn person in the whole fucking world, okay? I'm doing it for me. Reynolds.
MARTIN. Then do it in Reynolds' bedroom — with the shades down.
REYNOLDS. My actors deserve an audience.
MARTIN. So did Marie Antoinette. We are doomed, Louie. And if you don't disinvite those critics, those creepy-crawly nit-picking snakes ... who've caused eczema and nervous tics among theatre people for centuries, I swear on my mother, the William Morris police will break into the theatre, I mean the church and arrest you and your organ.
REYNOLDS. *(Jumps up pacing and weeping.)* I can't believe this. I cannot believe this. You ...
MARTIN. Wait-wait-what'd I say? Reynolds?
REYNOLDS. Fuck. You. You hear me? I ... I will sit alone ... in an empty theatre every night for two months to watch my actors all by myself if necessary. I don't care how bad you or anyone else thinks it is. I only wanted to be alone with your work, like a ... like a believer in the temple of your mind and why shouldn't I, when I paid for the whole production with my own fucking money?
MARTIN. Rule number one. Never invest your own mon ...
REYNOLDS. What do I give a shit about money? What's money to me when I'm on my way outta here?
MARTIN. Out-out. Out to whe ... where?
REYNOLDS. I had pneumonia last winter and ...
MARTIN. Well you're all right now.
REYNOLDS. No. Now I ... I ... have lumps. Lumps here, lumps here. So I ...
MARTIN. *(Overlap.)* Lumps, you have lumps ... like...?
REYNOLDS. ... cashed in my life insurance policy ...
MARTIN. *(Overlap.)* Lumps?
REYNOLDS. Yes. And they advanced ...
MARTIN. *(Overlap.)* Don't say it!
REYNOLDS. ... me two hundred thousand ...

MARTIN. No! You could have *done* something with that money ...

REYNOLDS. I am doing something.

MARTIN. I mean for *yourself!* — the new drugs.

REYNOLDS. They don't work on me. So what should I do? Go round the world on the QE-2 and get Legionnaires disease? Or into therapy with Elizabeth Kubler-Ross and Jack Kevorkian? All I ever dreamed of was to direct a play of yours. That is my crime. And why is it a crime to fulfill the deepest wish of ones life? I love the theatre. I love your work. It has tenderness and courage and ... and a beautiful message.

MARTIN. *(So stunned he almost cannot speak.)* All of my life I've been waiting to hear this.

REYNOLDS. But it doesn't count 'cause I'm only stupid me. You'd rather some psychotic critic ...

MARTIN. No no no. I'm unbearably touched. Believe me.

REYNOLDS. So I made a mistake and invited them. I paid for the license. The actors await my notes. I have your number upstate and I'll call you after the show. *(He's leaving the stage.)*

MARTIN. *Wait! I haven't told you the good things! (Reynolds freezes, turns.)*

REYNOLDS. What good things?

MARTIN. The dance. Loved the dance. God! The dance!

REYNOLDS. I cut it.

MARTIN. Oh thank God — I mean — you know best. But you lit the whole second act with one candle? What was that?

REYNOLDS. We blew a fuse.

MARTIN. Oh.

REYNOLDS. And when we went to change it, the fuse box, like exploded on us. Lucky we found a candle.

MARTIN. Luck Keee!

REYNOLDS. So what other good things?

MARTIN. The curtain call. I was stunned ...

REYNOLDS. I choreographed it.

MARTIN. Incredible.

REYNOLDS. It was hard work.

MARTIN. It showed. It showed.

REYNOLDS.   Is there a way I can call you tonight, like eleven?

MARTIN.   Sure. Call anytime.

REYNOLDS.   What about your wife?

MARTIN.   What wife?

REYNOLDS.   She can't breathe. She's choking.

MARTIN.   Oh. Actually I … have no wife.

REYNOLDS.   Oh. Are you really on this bus?

MARTIN.   Oh that I am. See? My ticket.

REYNOLDS.   How much did it cost?

MARTIN.   It's always a playwright's last twenty bucks for a bus ticket like this one.

REYNOLDS.   *(Throws down a pack of hundreds.)* Take this. Come with me. We can fix it. Whatever you want we'll do. Tons, tons of money. Here …

MARTIN.   This is fake money. Say this is fake mon …

REYNOLDS.   It's real and it's shit. Money is shit.

MARTIN.   I can't take this much real shit … money from you.

REYNOLDS.   I can't use it where I'm going. *(He's stuffing it in Martin's pockets.)* Pay your mortgage. Put on an extension. Don't you understand? You can't lose. You might even like your play.

MARTIN.   No no. This is putting my head into the tiger's mouth.

REYNOLDS.   The tiger will lap it up. You're an *author.* Where do you think the word "author" comes from? *Authority!* Give those critics the back of your hand and they'll fall on their knees and lick your feet.

MARTIN.   No. You don't know them. They never lick your feet.

REYNOLDS.   *(Overlap.) So forget 'em!*

MARTIN.   No no no. You don't under … – I–can–never–for-get–them–never–never.

REYNOLDS.   Just say: "I can forget the bastards."

MARTIN.   How can I say I can forget the bastards?

REYNOLDS.   You just … *did!*

MARTIN.   Huh? No. No. Wait. That's right. I did.

REYNOLDS.   Again now.

MARTIN.   That's right. I can ...

REYNOLDS.   I can forget ...

MARTIN.   I can *forget* the bastards. I *can* forget the *bastards*. *(Repeatedly.)* I can ... *(The Waiter comes out with a menu to take Reynolds' order. Martin keeps mumbling, repeating.)*

WAITER.   May I help you?

REYNOLDS.   *(Regarding the Waiter who is slovenly and like a slug.)* I don't think so. Wait — yeahhhh. Come to the play. Me director. Him playwright. Big hit Baby. What's your name?

WAITER.   James your waiter.

REYNOLDS.   What's he owe you? Ten? twenty? A hundred? *(Throws money down.)*

WAITER.   Oh that's too much.

REYNOLDS.   Come to his play. You'll love it. *(He hands the Waiter a poster. Martin and Reynolds leave. The Waiter unrolls the poster. His words fade under bright music.)*

WAITER.   Hey. Ya never know.

END

NEW PLAYS

★ **THE CREDEAUX CANVAS by Keith Bunin.** A forged painting leads to tragedy among friends. "There is that moment between adolescence and middle age when being disaffected looks attractive. Witness the enduring appeal of Prince Hamlet, Jake Barnes and James Dean, on the stage, page and screen. Or, more immediately, take a look at the lithe young things in THE CREDEAUX CANVAS..." –*NY Times.* "THE CREDEAUX CANVAS is the third recent play about painters...it turned out to be the best of the lot, better even than most plays about non-painters." –*NY Magazine.* [2M, 2W] ISBN: 0-8222-1838-0

★ **THE DIARY OF ANNE FRANK by Frances Goodrich and Albert Hackett, newly adapted by Wendy Kesselman.** A transcendently powerful new adaptation in which Anne Frank emerges from history a living, lyrical, intensely gifted young girl. "Undeniably moving. It shatters the heart. The evening never lets us forget the inhuman darkness waiting to claim its incandescently human heroine." –*NY Times.* "A sensitive, stirring and thoroughly engaging new adaptation." –*NY Newsday.* "A powerful new version that moves the audience to gasps, then tears." –*A.P.* "One of the year's ten best." –*Time Magazine.* [5M, 5W, 3 extras] ISBN: 0-8222-1718-X

★ **THE BOOK OF LIZ by David Sedaris and Amy Sedaris.** Sister Elizabeth Donderstock makes the cheese balls that support her religious community, but feeling unappreciated among the Squeamish, she decides to try her luck in the outside world. "...[a] delightfully off-key, off-color hymn to clichés we all live by, whether we know it or not." –*NY Times.* "Good-natured, goofy and frequently hilarious..." –*NY Newsday.* "...[THE BOOK OF LIZ] may well be the world's first Amish picaresque...hilarious..." –*Village Voice.* [2M, 2W (doubling, flexible casting to 8M, 7W)] ISBN: 0-8222-1827-5

★ **JAR THE FLOOR by Cheryl L. West.** A quartet of black women spanning four generations makes up this hilarious and heartwarming dramatic comedy. "...a moving and hilarious account of a black family sparring in a Chicago suburb..." –*NY Magazine.* "...heart-to-heart confrontations and surprising revelations...first-rate..." –*NY Daily News.* "...unpretentious good feelings...bubble through West's loving and humorous play..." –*Star-Ledger.* "...one of the wisest plays I've seen in ages...[from] a master playwright." –*USA Today.* [5W] ISBN: 0-8222-1809-7

★ **THIEF RIVER by Lee Blessing.** Love between two men over decades is explored in this incisive portrait of coming to terms with who you are. "Mr. Blessing unspools the plot ingeniously, skipping back and forth in time as the details require...an absorbing evening." –*NY Times.* "...wistful and sweet-spirited..." –*Variety.* [6M] ISBN: 0-8222-1839-9

★ **THE BEGINNING OF AUGUST by Tom Donaghy.** When Jackie's wife abruptly and mysteriously leaves him and their infant daughter, a pungently comic reevaluation of suburban life ensues. "Donaghy holds a cracked mirror up to the contemporary American family, anatomizing its frailties and miscommunications in fractured language that can be both funny and poignant." –*The Philadelphia Inquirer.* "...[A] sharp, eccentric new comedy. Pungently funny...fresh and precise..." –*LA Times.* [3M, 2W] ISBN: 0-8222-1786-4

★ **OUTSTANDING MEN'S MONOLOGUES 2001–2002 and OUTSTANDING WOMEN'S MONOLOGUES 2001–2002 edited by Craig Pospisil.** Drawn exclusively from Dramatists Play Service publications, these collections for actors feature over fifty monologues each and include an enormous range of voices, subject matter and characters. MEN'S ISBN: 0-8222-1821-6 WOMEN'S ISBN: 0-8222-1822-4

DRAMATISTS PLAY SERVICE, INC.
440 Park Avenue South, New York, NY 10016 212-683-8960 Fax 212-213-1539
postmaster@dramatists.com www.dramatists.com

NEW PLAYS

★ **A LESSON BEFORE DYING by Romulus Linney, based on the novel by Ernest J. Gaines.** An innocent young man is condemned to death in backwoods Louisiana and must learn to die with dignity. "The story's wrenching power lies not in its outrage but in the almost inexplicable grace the characters must muster as their only resistance to being treated like lesser beings." –*The New Yorker.* "Irresistable momentum and a cathartic explosion...a powerful inevitability." –*NY Times.* [5M, 2W] ISBN: 0-8222-1785-6

★ **BOOM TOWN by Jeff Daniels.** A searing drama mixing small-town love, politics and the consequences of betrayal. "...a brutally honest, contemporary foray into classic themes, exploring what moves people to lie, cheat, love and dream. By BOOM TOWN's climactic end there are no secrets, only bare truth." –*Oakland Press.* "...some of the most electrifying writing Daniels has ever done..." –*Ann Arbor News.* [2M, 1W] ISBN: 0-8222-1760-0

★ **INCORRUPTIBLE by Michael Hollinger.** When a motley order of medieval monks learns their patron saint no longer works miracles, a larcenous, one-eyed minstrel shows them an outrageous new way to pay old debts. "A lightning-fast farce, rich in both verbal and physical humor." –*American Theatre.* "Everything fits snugly in this funny, endearing black comedy...an artful blend of the mock-formal and the anachronistically breezy...A piece of remarkably dexterous craftsmanship." –*Philadelphia Inquirer.* "A farcical romp, scintillating and irreverent." –*Philadelphia Weekly.* [5M, 3W] ISBN: 0-8222-1787-2

★ **CELLINI by John Patrick Shanley.** Chronicles the life of the original "Renaissance Man," Benvenuto Cellini, the sixteenth-century Italian sculptor and man-about-town. Adapted from the autobiography of Benvenuto Cellini, translated by J. Addington Symonds. "[Shanley] has created a convincing Cellini, not neglecting his dark side, and a trim, vigorous, fast-moving show." –*BackStage.* "Very entertaining...With brave purpose, the narrative undermines chronology before untangling it...touching and funny..." –*NY Times.* [7M, 2W (doubling)] ISBN: 0-8222-1808-9

★ **PRAYING FOR RAIN by Robert Vaughan.** Examines a burst of fatal violence and its aftermath in a suburban high school. "Thought provoking and compelling." –*Denver Post.* "Vaughan's powerful drama offers hope and possibilities." –*Theatre.com.* "[The play] doesn't put forth compact, tidy answers to the problem of youth violence. What it does offer is a compelling exploration of the forces that influence an individual's choices, and of the proverbial lifelines—be they familial, communal, religious or political—that tragically slacken when society gives in to apathy, fear and self-doubt..." –*Westword.* "...a symphony of anger..." –*Gazette Telegraph.* [4M, 3W] ISBN: 0-8222-1807-0

★ **GOD'S MAN IN TEXAS by David Rambo.** When a young pastor takes over one of the most prestigious Baptist churches from a rip-roaring old preacher-entrepreneur, all hell breaks loose. "...the pick of the litter of all the works at the Humana Festival..." –*Providence Journal.* "...a wealth of both drama and comedy in the struggle for power..." –*LA Times.* "...the first act is so funny...deepens in the second act into a sobering portrait of fear, hope and self-delusion..." –*Columbus Dispatch.* [3M] ISBN: 0-8222-1801-1

★ **JESUS HOPPED THE 'A' TRAIN by Stephen Adly Guirgis.** A probing, intense portrait of lives behind bars at Rikers Island. "...fire-breathing...whenever it appears that JESUS is settling into familiar territory, it slides right beneath expectations into another, fresher direction. It has the courage of its intellectual restlessness...[JESUS HOPPED THE 'A' TRAIN] has been written in flame." –*NY Times.* [4M, 1W] ISBN: 0-8222-1799-6

DRAMATISTS PLAY SERVICE, INC.
440 Park Avenue South, New York, NY 10016 212-683-8960 Fax 212-213-1539
postmaster@dramatists.com www.dramatists.com

NEW PLAYS

★ **THE CIDER HOUSE RULES, PARTS 1 & 2 by Peter Parnell, adapted from the novel by John Irving.** Spanning eight decades of American life, this adaptation from the Irving novel tells the story of Dr. Wilbur Larch, founder of the St. Cloud's, Maine orphanage and hospital, and of the complex father-son relationship he develops with the young orphan Homer Wells. "...luxurious digressions, confident pacing...an enterprise of scope and vigor..." –*NY Times*. "...The fact that I can't wait to see Part 2 only begins to suggest just how good it is..." –*NY Daily News*. "...engrossing...an odyssey that has only one major shortcoming: It comes to an end." –*Seattle Times*. "...outstanding...captures the humor, the humility...of Irving's 588-page novel..." –*Seattle Post-Intelligencer*. [9M, 10W, doubling, flexible casting] PART 1 ISBN: 0-8222-1725-2 PART 2 ISBN: 0-8222-1726-0

★ **TEN UNKNOWNS by Jon Robin Baitz.** An iconoclastic American painter in his seventies has his life turned upside down by an art dealer and his ex-boyfriend. "...breadth and complexity...a sweet and delicate harmony rises from the four cast members...Mr. Baitz is without peer among his contemporaries in creating dialogue that spontaneously conveys a character's social context and moral limitations..." –*NY Times*. "...darkly funny, brilliantly desperate comedy...TEN UNKNOWNS vibrates with vital voices." –*NY Post*. [3M, 1W] ISBN: 0-8222-1826-7

★ **BOOK OF DAYS by Lanford Wilson.** A small-town actress playing St. Joan struggles to expose a murder. "...[Wilson's] best work since *Fifth of July*...An intriguing, prismatic and thoroughly engrossing depiction of contemporary small-town life with a murder mystery at its core...a splendid evening of theater..." –*Variety*. "...fascinating...a densely populated, unpredictable little world." –*St. Louis Post-Dispatch*. [6M, 5W] ISBN: 0-8222-1767-8

★ **THE SYRINGA TREE by Pamela Gien.** Winner of the 2001 Obie Award. A breathtakingly beautiful tale of growing up white in apartheid South Africa. "Instantly engaging, exotic, complex, deeply shocking...a thoroughly persuasive transport to a time and a place...stun[s] with the power of a gut punch..." –*NY Times*. "Astonishing...affecting ...[with] a dramatic and heartbreaking conclusion...A deceptive sweet simplicity haunts THE SYRINGA TREE..." –*A.P.* [1W (or flexible cast)] ISBN: 0-8222-1792-9

★ **COYOTE ON A FENCE by Bruce Graham.** An emotionally riveting look at capital punishment. "The language is as precise as it is profane, provoking both troubling thought and the occasional cheerful laugh...will change you a little before it lets go of you." –*Cincinnati CityBeat*. "...excellent theater in every way..." –*Philadelphia City Paper*. [3M, 1W] ISBN: 0-8222-1738-4

★ **THE PLAY ABOUT THE BABY by Edward Albee.** Concerns a young couple who have just had a baby and the strange turn of events that transpire when they are visited by an older man and woman. "An invaluable self-portrait of sorts from one of the few genuinely great living American dramatists...rockets into that special corner of theater heaven where words shoot off like fireworks into dazzling patterns and hues." –*NY Times*. "An exhilarating, wicked...emotional terrorism." –*NY Newsday*. [2M, 2W] ISBN: 0-8222-1814-3

★ **FORCE CONTINUUM by Kia Corthron.** Tensions among black and white police officers and the neighborhoods they serve form the backdrop of this discomfiting look at life in the inner city. "The creator of this intense...new play is a singular voice among American playwrights...exceptionally eloquent..." –*NY Times*. "...a rich subject and a wise attitude." –*NY Post*. [6M, 2W, 1 boy] ISBN: 0-8222-1817-8

DRAMATISTS PLAY SERVICE, INC.
440 Park Avenue South, New York, NY 10016 212-683-8960 Fax 212-213-1539
postmaster@dramatists.com www.dramatists.com